BREAKING THE CYCLE

ISSUES AFFECTING POVERTY

CATHY BUTLER

Woman's Missionary Union
Birmingham, Alabama

Woman's Missionary Union
P. O. Box 830010
Birmingham, AL 35283-0010

For more information, visit our Web site at www.wmu.com or call 1-800-968-7301.

Dewey Decimal Classification: 261.8
Subject Headings: POVERTY
                   CHURCH AND SOCIAL PROBLEMS

Unless otherwise indicated, Scripture quotations are from the Holy Bible, *New International Version* (NIV). Copyright © 1973, 1978, 1984 International Bible Society. Used by permission of Zondervan Bible Publishers.

Scripture quotations identified KJV are from the King James Version of the Bible.

Scripture quotations identified CEV are from *Contemporary English Version.* Copyright © American Bible Society 1991. Used by permission.

Scripture quotations identified TEV are from the *Good News Bible,* Today's English Version. Old Testament: © American Bible Society, 1976; New Testament: © American Bible Society, 1966, 1971, 1976.

Scripture quotations identified NKJV are from the New King James Version. Copyright © 1982 by Thomas Nelson, Inc. Used by permission. All rights reserved.

Cover Design by Theresa Barnett
Design by Janell E. Young

ISBN: 1-56309- 893-8
W043104•0504•2M1

CONTENTS

1

THE BIBLICAL MANDATE TO ADDRESS POVERTY

"'The blind receive their sight and the lame walk; the lepers are cleansed and the deaf hear; the dead are raised up and the poor have the gospel preached to them'" (Matt. 11:5 NKJV).

"'The Spirit of the Lord is upon Me, because he has anointed me to preach the gospel to the poor. He has sent Me to heal the brokenhearted, to preach liberation of the captives and recovery of sight to the blind, to set at liberty those who are oppressed, to preach the acceptable year of the Lord'" (Luke 4:18–19 NKJV).

When Jesus stood in His hometown to declare His ministry, He said He was anointed to preach the gospel to the poor—literally, to bring them good news. When John the Baptist, then Herod's prisoner, needed reassurance of Jesus' identity, Jesus said, "Tell him the poor have good news preached to them." The poor were not an afterthought with Jesus; they were central to His ministry. He gave them good news by giving them Himself. He healed their bodies, fed them, blessed their children, visited with them, and taught them to put their faith in God rather than the world.

The poor desperately needed the ministry of Jesus, for first-century Jewish society had fallen away from God's standards for relating to the poor as laid down in the laws of Moses, the wisdom writings, and the Prophets. Jesus' ministry to the poor seemed revolutionary at the time, but He was actually trying to bring society back to the fair and just society God had designed for His people.

God's first commands in Exodus dealing with the problem of poverty are not about how much to give the poor or under what circumstances they should be given assistance. God's first concern was and still is to make sure the poor are treated justly.

"'You shall not pervert the judgment of your poor in his dispute'" (Ex. 23:6 NKJV).

"'You shall do no injustice in judgment. You shall not be partial to the poor, nor honor the person of the mighty. But in righteousness you shall judge your neighbor'" (Lev. 19:15 NKJV).

Though it was possible a judge could have been moved to rule unfairly in favor of the poor, it was much more likely that a judge would show partiality to the rich and powerful. God did not want justice perverted in either direction. If God's commands had been obeyed, there would have been no poor underclass. Knowing the human heart, God gave commands to protect the poor from abuse, such as this command about charging interest:

"'If you lend money to any of My people who are poor among you, you shall not be like a moneylender to him; you shall not charge him interest'" (Ex. 22:25 NKJV).

The whole concept of Jubilee (Lev. 25:8–17) is based on God's economic plan. Debts would be canceled, land returned to the original owner, and slaves freed. Everyone would more or less go back to the beginning. But with a plan like that, how could anyone hope to build a great fortune? It couldn't be done, which was the point. God's people would focus on serving God rather than wealth.

Jubilee was to come every 49th year, though there is no evidence the Israelites ever obeyed God by observing Jubilee. Every 7th year, however, the farmland was to lie fallow (meaning no crops were raised on it). God specifically commanded that whatever grew of its own accord that year was to be for the poor and for the wild animals.

"'But the seventh year you shall let it rest and lie fallow, that the poor of your people may eat; and what they leave, the beasts of the field may eat. In like manner you shall do with your vineyard and your olive grove'" (Ex. 23:11 NKJV).

This 7th year was a gleaning year, but God instituted the practice of gleaning on a regular basis.

"'And you shall not glean your vineyard, nor shall you gather every grape of your vineyard; you shall leave them for the poor and the stranger: I am the Lord your God'" (Lev. 19:10 NKJV).

When farmers would gather the crops, some would always be missed, or not yet ripe. God did not allow the farmer to go back and get those scraps—they were for the poor.

According to Bible scholars, the practice of leaving the gleanings was a pre-Israelite practice; but whereas the Canaanites left the gleanings as an offering for the nature spirits, God intended them to be for the weakest and most dependent of His people. The phrase "I am the Lord your God" is not just a catchphrase, but relates directly to Lev. 19:1 (NKJV): "'You shall be holy; for I the Lord your God am holy.'" The Israelites' treatment of the poor was to be a direct reflection of the character of their God: just, kind, and caring. Today, the way Christians relate to the poor is also to be a reflection of the character of our God. "The Bible consistently shows that human morality is ultimately justified by the nature of God."[1]

Even with such laws, it would happen that someone would fall into poverty through bad choices, or circumstances such as sickness or accident. God's mandate for relating to the poor went beyond the negative commands of "Do not be partial; do not charge interest." God's people are to respond in a loving, positive way.

"'If one of your brethren becomes poor, and falls into poverty among you, then you shall help him, like a stranger or a sojourner, that he may live with you'" (Lev. 25:35 NKJV).

God had made it abundantly clear to His people that the stranger (alien, immigrant, visitor) among them was to be treated fairly. Had they not been strangers in Egypt (Ex. 23:9)? Their own poor brethren deserved to be treated just as well.

Although God planned a just and fair society, He knew some portion of the people would always be poor (Deut. 15:11). He wanted generosity and tenderness shown to them. God warned against being hard-hearted and tight-fisted toward the poor.

"'If there is among you a poor man of your brethren, within any of the gates in your land which the Lord your God is giving you, you shall not harden your heart nor shut your hand from your poor brother, but you shall open your hand wide to him *and willingly lend him sufficient for his need, whatever he needs'"* (Deut. 15:7–8 NKJV).

As the Israelites developed their own nation, complete with a king, the mandate to care for the poor and treat them with justice continued to be taught, although many of God's specific commands were ignored. The Psalms and Proverbs both contained references to the poor. Psalms promised God's care for the poor:

"For He shall stand at the right hand of the poor, to save him from those who condemn him" (Psalm 109:31 NKJV).

Proverbs, with its emphasis on human behavior, compared the righteous who treated the poor fairly with the wicked who couldn't even comprehend the plight of the poor.

"The righteous considers the cause of the poor, but the wicked does not understand such knowledge" (Prov. 29:7 NKJV).

As the years passed and Israel cared more for the form of religion than an actual relationship with God, the teachings of justice for the poor became lost to all but a handful of the faithful. God sent prophets to call the people back to obedience—an obedience that included justice for the poor.

When Amos confronted the Jews with their sins of idol worship, selfishness, and corruption, he singled out women who were willing for the poor to suffer if that suffering allowed them to live in luxury (Amos 4:1). In Amos 5:10–12, the prophet predicts God's judgment specifically upon those who oppressed the poor and perverted justice so that the poor had no recourse. Though the religious leaders observed the rules of offerings and feast days, their behavior toward the poor made their religious activities repulsive to the God of justice. Instead God commanded, *"'But let justice run down like water, and righteousness like a mighty stream'"* (Amos 5:24 NKJV).

Amos 8 paints a vivid picture of the destruction awaiting those who "swallow up the needy, and make the poor of the land fail" (Amos 8:4 NKJV). These were not people who literally broke into the homes of the poor and took what little they had. They were religious and political officials who wanted the poor to bear the burden of paying most of the taxes, even if that meant that the poor must go hungry. They were merchants who used false scales to cheat those who bought and sold grain, who were impatient for the holy days to be over so they could buy and sell. They even plotted to sell wheat they knew was no good (Amos 8:5–6).

The practices that oppressed the poor then were typical of a rural, farm economy. The more urban life of the twenty-first century offers many other ways to cheat the poor. The modern counterparts of the people Amos condemned still use unfair tax systems; but instead of rigged scales, they may use rigged legal documents or accounting practices. Instead of bad wheat they may sell defective products or substandard houses.

Oppression of the poor happens on a grand scale, but also on a personal one. Imagine a woman who tells her housekeeper, "I don't have any cash to pay you your salary this week. I'll get it to you next week." She doesn't stop to think, or perhaps doesn't care, that the housekeeper was counting on that money to buy food for her family. What difference does it make to her, as long as she enjoys the housekeeper's labor and is not inconvenienced?

Israel ignored the warnings of the prophets, and suffered God's chastisement. God had not forgotten His people, however; and hundreds of years after Amos, God came in the flesh to live among humankind and teach them many things, including how to love and care for the poor among them.

JESUS AND THE POOR

As seen at the beginning of this chapter, Jesus proclaimed that part of His purpose on earth was to preach good news to the poor. By the time of Jesus' ministry, many religious people believed those who were sick or poor were under the judgment of God, while He singled out the wealthy and privileged for special blessings. This health-and-wealth heresy is still currently taught in some circles today.

So it was revolutionary for Jesus to pay so much attention to, and put so much emphasis upon, the poor and their needs. He did this by preaching of God's forgiveness, telling them of the kingdom of heaven, feeding them, visiting with them, and healing them. While some that Jesus healed, such as the centurion's servant and Jairus's daughter, were not poor, others had become impoverished through their illness, such as the woman with the issue of blood who had spent all she had on doctors. Others, it can be assumed, could not afford medical treatment. Regardless of their social condition, Jesus healed them. He also healed people regardless of what His critics thought. In Luke 14:1–6, He healed a man on the Sabbath. Not only did religious leaders disapprove of healing on the Sabbath because it was considered work, but the man had dropsy, an excess of body fluids. This painful condition was believed at the time to be a sign of sexual immorality in the sufferer. So Jesus not only dared heal someone, He healed a man whom others saw as justly suffering for his sins. (It is not difficult to see the parallel between this situation and the attitude of some Christians toward people with AIDS.)

When Jesus healed the sick and fed the hungry, He did so because He was moved with compassion for them. Matthew 15:32–39 tells of Jesus feeding the crowd of 4,000. He specifically said He did not want to send people away hungry because "I have compassion on the multitude." Does this mean we are required only to minister to those for whom we feel emotion? While many appeals to help the poor are based on moving the listener to pity, ministry cannot be based upon emotion. Ministry is based upon obedience to the biblical mandate. Jesus, sharing the heart of God, was acting in the character of God, which is compassionate. As we minister in obedience—whether we feel like ministering or not—we will develop that kind of compassion.

Finally, Jesus made ministry to the poor one of the identifying marks of His followers. He tells them that at judgment He will divide out everyone before him.

"'Then the king will say to those on His right hand, "Come, you blessed of My Father, inherit the kingdom prepared for you from the foundation of the world: for I was hungry and you gave Me food; I was thirsty and you gave Me drink; I was a stranger and you took Me in; I was naked and you clothed Me; I was sick and you visited Me; I was in prison and you came to Me"'" (Matt. 25:33–36 NKJV).

The righteous will then wonder and ask when they did these things for Jesus. His answer will be:

"'Assuredly, I say to you, inasmuch as you did it to one of the least of these My brethren, you did it to Me'" (Matt. 25:40 NKJV).

Jesus is not saying that faith in Him is not central to salvation, but those who truly believe in Him, who live with the Holy Spirit within them, will act as Jesus acted. When they ministered to the poor, the needy, and the afflicted, they were ministering to Jesus. That's how important ministry to the poor is in the sight of God.

Not long after Jesus gives this teaching, He stopped at Bethany to visit in the house of Simon, a leper. Again, Jesus was breaking with tradition by associating with a leper. Then a woman came in and anointed His head with costly ointment. This was a beautiful act of devotion that Jesus honored, but the men around Jesus grumbled that she had wasted the oil. It could have been sold and the money used to help the poor. Mark 14:5 (NKJV) says, "And they criticized her sharply." This criticism indicates several things; among them that Jesus had taught His disciples well about stewardship and sacrifice for the poor. Many have distorted Jesus' answer, however. The fragment of verse 7 is often quoted out of context: "'For you have the poor with you always'" as if Jesus were saying there is no point trying to address poverty; it is eternal. This is not at all what Jesus said. The full verse reads: "'For you have the poor with you always, *and whenever you wish you may do them good*; but Me you do not have always'" (Mark 14:7 [NKJV]; *author's italics*).

The woman was honoring Jesus while she could, while He was with her. Now Jesus is not with us in the flesh; we can still honor Him, precisely by ministering to the poor.

THE EARLY CHURCH AND THE POOR

After Jesus' ascension, the early church continued His teachings of care for the poor. But as the church became more organized, there developed the type of administrative questions that any organization must face. Who would receive ministry? How would it be funded? Who would administer the care? Those who preached and taught could not do everything (as any church staff member today will attest). Laypeople were needed to care for those who needed help, and rules were laid down to determine who would receive help. For example, those with widowed mothers were to support their mothers rather than expect the church to do so; but older widows with no family to turn to could expect to look to the church for assistance. It was part of honoring one's mother to provide for her in her old age. It was part of caring for the poor to provide for those who had nowhere else to turn.

The elders of the church wanted believers to know that not only were they to care for the poor, they were to do so willingly, even joyfully.

"But whoever has this world's goods, and sees his brother in need, and shuts up his heart from him, how does the love of God abide in him? My little children, let us not love in word or in tongue, but in deed and in truth" (1 John 3:17–18 NKJV).

It should be remembered that not only had Jewish society accepted the idea that the poor were being punished by God, but many believers who came from a non-Jewish background had no concept of responsibility to the poor whatsoever. While Jews had the witness of the prophets and the Mosaic law, people coming from a pagan background had no framework of justice and compassion. The teachings of the early church on not showing partiality and promoting justice were an extension of the Mosaic teachings and familiar to Jewish believers. They were new to many Gentile believers, and had to be emphasized and explained, as in James 2.

In James 2 believers are reminded not to show favoritism to the rich who come to their assembly, to the point that the poor are forced to give up their seats to the rich. Yet often the rich were the same ones who dragged believers into court and blasphemed the name of Jesus. James reminded his readers that God had chosen the poor of the world to be "rich in faith and heirs of the kingdom which He promised to those who love Him" (James 2:5 NKJV). There was no spiritual underclass for the poor—in God's design, they were spiritually equal with their wealthier brothers and sisters in Christ.

Throughout church history, Christians have been on the forefront of changing society with hospitals, schools, orphanages, and other institutions to minister to the poor and those in need. Now, for a variety of reasons, the church is sometimes running behind society; observe the church's slow response to the AIDS epidemic. Now we run the risk of needing the world to lead us to the areas of great human need, rather than taking the lead in transforming our culture by ministering to the poor in the name of Christ. When those who do not know Christ do a better job of championing justice and bestowing mercy than do Christ followers, the church's witness to the gospel is damaged and weakened.

Through ministries such as the ones described in this book, the church can obey the biblical mandate of addressing poverty, treating the poor with justice, and sharing with them the good news that Jesus brought to us all.

---

[1]Clifton J. Allen, ed., *Broadman Bible Commentary* (Nashville: Broadman Press, 1970), 2:51.

2

THE SCOPE OF POVERTY

"The rich and the poor have this in common, the Lord is the maker of them all" (Prov. 22:2 NKJV).

Who determines what makes a person poor in the material sense? There are at least two ways of looking at poverty—one is a subjective approach, using feelings, opinions, and personal experiences. With the subjective approach, a person with $10 million might think a person with a net worth of $100,000 was poor. On the other hand, a person living in a cardboard box under a bridge would think the person with $100,000 to be fantastically rich. One's personal experiences and attitude toward life affect one's idea of poverty. We each have a subjective view of poverty, and it can change radically with new experiences.

For example, a Christian couple who lived in a modest two-bedroom apartment and drove old cars considered themselves lower middle class. When they took in a foster child, however, they quickly realized that she had a different view. She thought, and said, they were rich. When they protested that they were far from wealthy she replied, "You are so because you always have enough to eat and there are no holes in your floors!" She gave them a new way of thinking about their economic standing.

But to really study and understand poverty, and make inroads in fighting it, there must be objective standards— statistics, numbers, levels, and so forth. When setting standards of poverty and wealth in the United States (US), the US Census Bureau measures poverty using the official US poverty measure.

According to the US Census Bureau, poverty is measured by taking into account income thresholds and family size. A threshold of a certain amount of income related to family size determines whether the family is poor. "If a family's total income is less than that family's threshold, then that family, and every individual in it, is considered poor." While setting income thresholds is necessary for making public policy, the federal government realizes it is not a perfect method. For one thing, the thresholds do not take the cost of living in different areas into account; yet the cost of living for a family in Silicon Valley, California, or New York City is very different from a rural family in Alaska or a suburban family in Cincinnati. It also does not count noncash benefits such as public housing and Medicaid, which improve a family's standard of living but not their cash income.

According to the Census Bureau, "While the thresholds in some sense represent families' needs, the official poverty measure should be interpreted as a statistical yardstick rather than as a complete description of what people and families need to live."

WHAT PEOPLE NEED TO LIVE

And what do people need to live? Food, clean water and air, shelter, safety, clothing, medical care—these are the very basics of physical existence. But what about other things that are beyond the reach of the poor—recreation, education, legal help, spiritual nurture? And there are intangibles such as beauty, hope, and joy, the things that make life meaningful rather than just an animal existence.

It has been said by many people, and is quite true, that before a person can attend to spiritual and emotional matters, that person must have certain physical needs met. In psychologist Abraham Maslow's famous hierarchy of needs, physical needs such as food and safety form the base of the pyramid. Then other things, such as self-actualization (becoming what you have the potential to become) can be pursued.

While this is true, we must remember that every model or construct or human truth, whatever you wish to call it, has limits. The limit of the idea that the poor must have physical needs met before spiritual needs can be attended to lies in the assumption that the poor are so beaten down physically, so obsessed with their next meal or next place to sleep, that they are without heart, soul, and mind. Or, at best, that their mental and spiritual faculties are dormant or stunted. It is true that millions of people have never reached their God-given potential because of poverty. But one need only look at the many great people who rose from poverty to see that the poor are capable of deep feeling and sensitivity. In some cases it is because of, rather than in spite of, their poverty that they were tenderhearted toward their fellow man. Could Charles Dickens have written *A Christmas Carol* or *Oliver Twist* if he had never known the pain of hunger and cold? And while there are few who have risen to the heights of a Dickens, there are many other poor who are quite capable of a sensitivity to beauty, of fearing what follows death, of dreaming dreams that go beyond food and clothing.

So the needs of the poor are material, but also mental, emotional, and spiritual. Jane Addams, the founder of the settlement house movement in the United States, realized this. She knew the poor and working classes needed education, skills, work, training in parenting and homemaking, counseling (known then as mental hygiene), and ample opportunities for rest and wholesome recreation. But she did not teach them that they should feel sorry for themselves. Telling the poor that they are morally superior because of their poverty plays well to the audience of the poor, but does nothing to help them.

Everyone feels they can't afford certain things, but must have them to be happy. When is this an inconvenience, and when is it a hardship? Suppose you are on the benevolence committee of your church. The church preschool director comes to you and asks the committee to pay for ballet lessons for a child in the school. She is the only little girl in her class who isn't taking ballet and she cries every day over it. Her parents are divorced. One parent can't afford the lessons, and the other won't pay for them. She does have food, clothing, a school, and a home. Do ballet lessons in this case qualify as benevolence?

What about the person who feels deprived because she doesn't own a microwave or DVD player? Or the parent who receives toys for her child from the church toy drive and then comes back complaining that her child didn't get the latest video game system? Some people would feel all these things were real needs and would want to meet them. Others would say they were luxuries and the person who lacked them could not be considered poor simply because of not owning them.

Some of these questions can only be decided one case at a time. So many things must be balanced. There is the pressure of our consumer society that says people must have the latest of everything to be happy and fulfilled. There is the idea that people need to take responsibility for their lives and not expect everything to be given to them. And there is also the balance between tangible and intangible needs. Perhaps the little girl who had many of life's good things but wanted ballet lessons needed to understand that we can't always have everything everyone else has, and it's OK to feel sad about it. But what if a teacher who had a talented student that lived in a slum and couldn't afford art lessons approached the same benevolence committee? The teacher feels art lessons might give this child from a poverty-stricken environment not only drawing skills but hope and a vision for a better personal future, a future that included beauty and creativity rather than squalor and destruction.

When considering the scope of poverty, such intangibles must be considered, and also some guidelines drawn. A church, ministry group, or individual must ask, "For the purposes of our outreach and ministry, what do we consider to be poverty? What will our ministry to the poor include in the way of physical, spiritual, social, and emotional care?" In the healthiest ministry settings, these questions will always be open for review as Christians learn more and more about how to show God's love to the poor.   *✳ diff. types/areas of poverty*

POVERTY IN THE UNITED STATES

Taking into account physical, mental, emotional, and spiritual needs, what is the scope of poverty in the United States? How many people are poor? Where are they? Who are they?

While it would be hard to imagine any city, town, or county that does not have poor people within it, some are well hidden from public view. Perhaps you have heard someone say, "I can't believe anybody in our town goes to bed hungry at night." Anyone who really wants to know if there is poverty in their area need only ask schoolteachers, emergency room workers, pastors, police officers, and firefighters. Sometimes even they might not know of the hidden poverty around them. Some poverty is so invisible that it is only when the poor person reaches out for help that it's seen.

One real-life example of this kind of discovery occurred when a church in an affluent suburb received a call from a woman asking if she could get a ride to the grocery store. She had food stamps, but her car had broken down. A church member went to get her. When she reached the address, she thought there must have been a mistake. An expensive foreign sports car was in the driveway of a large house on a secluded lot. Surely no poor person lived there! As she started to leave, a young woman ran from the house and flagged her down. She explained that she was the person who needed help. She house-sat for the absent owner. He allowed her to live in the home, but she was paid almost no money and had to feed herself and her child as best she could. She was certain none of the neighbors realized her plight. If she had not reached out for help and if the church had not responded, how would anyone have known the depth of her need?

Those who make public policy cannot rely only on stories like this, which they refer to as anecdotal evidence. They need a broader picture, which the US Census provides. The following facts come from the 2000 Census Supplementary Survey. In that year:
- 9.57 percent of households had incomes below $10,000
- 6.68 percent of households had incomes of $10,000–$14,999
- 13.36 percent of households had incomes of $15,000–$24,999

How is household defined? (# in household)

The picture hasn't improved. In a census report on poverty rates from 2001 to 2002, it was found that the official poverty rate in 2002 was 12.1 percent, up from 11.7 percent in 2001. This comes to 34.6 million people, 1.7 million more than were in poverty only a year earlier. Breaking it down by ages for adults, the rates for the elderly poor remained unchanged at 10.4 percent, or 3.4 to 3.6 million people. The rates for those aged 18 to 64 years old increased from 10.1 percent to 10.6. This is an increase from 17.8 million people to 18.9 million people.

For families, the rate increased from 9.2 percent in 2001 to 9.6 percent the next year. This means instead of 6.8 million poor families, America had 7.2 million poor families. Female-headed households had a stable poverty rate of 26.5 percent, but numbers increased from 3.5 million to 3.6 million.

The picture for the poor children of America is bleak. According to the census figures, while the poverty rates for children stayed the same from 2001 to 2002 at 16.7 percent, the number of children in poverty rose from 11.7 million in 2001 to 12.1 million in 2002. The report stated, "Children under 6 have been particularly vulnerable to poverty." The lack of a father in the household had a great effect on the poverty level. Of children under age 6 living in families headed by a female householder with no male present, 48.6 percent lived in poverty. This compares to a poverty rate of 9.7 percent for young children in a household headed by a married couple. The poverty rate increased fivefold for fatherless children.

Children live in poverty in rates disproportionate to their presence in American society. Children make up one-fourth of the country's population, but they make up 35.1 percent of its poor. Many of these children are "severely poor"—their families live at *half* the poverty threshold.

Poverty is no respecter of race. According to the census report, the poverty rate among Hispanics was unchanged at 21.8 percent. For non-Hispanic whites, the poverty rate stayed at 8 percent. For Asians, the rate also stayed the same at 10 to 10.3 percent, depending on the definition of race of the various Asian populations. For black Americans, the poverty rate went from 22.7 percent in 2001 to 23.9–24.1 percent, depending on definitions of race. (Statistics for race were complicated by the fact respondents can now claim more than one race.)

Every region of the country is affected by poverty, but none more than the South. With 35.6 percent of the nation's population, the South has 40.6 percent of its poor. The rates of poverty stayed the same in 2001 and 2002 in the Northeast (10.9 percent) and the West (12.4 percent). It rose in the Midwest from 9.4 percent to 10.3 percent.

Poverty can be found in every area of the country: the suburbs as well as the inner city, rural farming country as well as college towns. Poverty stretches from the Rio Grande river valley to the Great Lakes region. It creates, and is in turn created by illiteracy, domestic instability, crime and incarceration, disease, racism, and mental illness. Ministries by Christians who are both compassionate toward the poor and dedicated to ministry can break the cycle of poverty's continual creation, renewal, and spread.

AROUND THE GLOBE

It's easy to think one knows about global poverty from sound bites on the evening news and heart-tugging commercials asking for help for "the children." Such understanding hardly touches the surface of global poverty. It can be found in both the industrialized and developing worlds; in rural areas; and in the booming, overburdened metropolitan centers.

Though poverty spawns the same ills in the rest of the world that it does in the United States, those ills can take different forms. While lack of preventive medical care plagues the poor of the US, infectious diseases such as malaria and HIV/AIDS ravage the poor populations of the world, especially Africa.

In the US, poor children are more likely to drop out of school or graduate with no real education. In developing countries, children, especially girls, are less likely to go to school at all.

While poverty causes families in the US to break up or go on government assistance, poverty in other countries can trap people into slavery. People sell themselves into slavery to pay debts; children are sold as prostitutes, farmhands, or factory workers.

In the US, 3.3 percent of households experience hunger. This usually means some or all the people in those households skip meals or eat too little. They go to bed hungry at night and wake up even hungrier the next morning. In the whole world, more than 840 million people are malnourished; of these, 153 million are less than 5 years old. Every day 31,000 children die from hunger and diseases caused by malnutrition.

Poverty also causes a health crisis around the globe. According to figures cited by the World Bank, each year 12 million people die from lack of clean water and water-borne diseases. Three-fourths of the world's population lives without wastewater disposal; almost 2.5 billion have no decent sanitation, and well over 1 billion have no clean water.

Is there really such a huge gap between the rich and poor? Aren't we all struggling to make ends meet? According to the Human Development Report 2002, "Deepening Democracy in a Fragmented World," the amount of money that the richest 1 percent of the world's people make annually equals what the poorest 57 percent make! The richest 5 percent of the world's people have incomes 114 times that of the poorest 5 percent. Of the 6.2 billion people in the world, 1.2 billion live on less than $1 a day. The next time you start feeling deprived, that might be a good fact to remember.

We have spent this chapter looking at a lot of theories, numbers, and statistics. Behind each of those dry statistics, however, is a living, breathing human being, a person with a heart, a mind, and a soul. These are people for whom Christ died. In the next chapters we will look at ways Christians are ministering to those people in the name of Christ.

3

WOMEN, CHILDREN, AND POVERTY

"While the media make us aware of the plight of America's children, the 'hot button' approach of focusing on only one issue at a time can give us a warped sense of reality."
Claudia Swain, Child Advocacy Resource Kit

The people most likely to suffer from poverty are women and children. Countless studies have borne out this fact, whether the women and children are in the United States or across the world in Bangladesh or Zimbabwe. It is a global fact.

Some reasons for this are that men are, in general, more free to abandon family responsibilities because not all countries have or enforce laws requiring them to support their children. Thus, providing for children falls to the women. Even in developed countries, women tend to make less money than men. In developing countries, jobs for women are scarce or nonexistent.

In many countries, men are forcibly removed from their families to fight in a war, and no support is given to their families. If they survive, when they return, they may be too disabled to work, or their job may have disappeared or their land been taken in their absence.

Another factor in the poverty of women and children is a cultural one—in some people groups women and children are not valued as much as men, so they receive less food, less education, less everything; but they are expected to work very hard. It's easy to think this is just a factor "over there" in some other part of the world, but many families in the United States also suffer from a "man-first, man-most" structure, though they might not admit to it publicly for fear of scorn or ridicule. Christianity has often been viewed as an antidote for this kind of attitude because it teaches care and support for everyone, especially children. Many male missionaries have testified that they are highly conscious of their role as husband and father and stand ready to explain to other men on their missions field why they show tenderness and regard for their wives and children.

There is also a practical reason for often giving the men or older boys the best food, the best education, and other resources in a family. The breadwinners have to have the physical stamina to go out and work. They also need the education to hold a job.

SLAVERY

One of the worst results of poverty among women and children is the likelihood of becoming an actual slave. According to iAbolish, the Anti-Slavery Portal, there are four main types of slavery today: sex slavery, forced labor, debt bondage, and chattel slavery. In 2003 it was estimated that 27 million people worldwide were enslaved. Many sex slaves are young girls sold by their male relatives to pay off debts to moneylenders or to relieve the family of the burden of their upkeep.

Forced labor entraps men, women, and children, who are frequently promised good jobs, then enslaved when they reach their workplace. The Central Intelligence Agency (CIA) estimates that each year in the US 50,000 women and children are trafficked as slaves: prostitutes, garment workers, domestics, and agricultural migrant workers. Only a small number are freed. A media campaign has made the world more aware of the enslavement of young boys on African cocoa plantations, the same plantations that provide the cocoa for the chocolate candy other children enjoy.

According to iAbolish's Web site, there are 15 to 20 million slaves in debt bondage in Bangladesh, India, Nepal, and Pakistan alone. These people have actually been used as collateral for a loan which they or someone in their families received.

Finally there is chattel slavery, which uses people as inheritable property. Though the 1927 Slavery Convention outlawed slavery worldwide, this system of passing along people as property or raiding villages for new slaves still exists, most prominently in Sudan and Mauritania. In Sudan, thousands of Christians have been enslaved by non-Christian tribes.

Would eradicating poverty end slavery? No. As long as there are people who want to have power over others, there will be oppression; but the types of slavery that depend on a person's poverty to make him or her passive or helpless could not flourish.

EDUCATION

Throughout this book, statistics and studies have been quoted that show a direct relationship between education and poverty. Much more data exists than could be quoted in one book, but here are a few more facts about how lack of education hurts the poor, especially children.

According to the National Institute for Literacy, in 1997, the poverty rate in the US for children under age 6 whose better-educated parent had less than a high school degree was a staggering 62.5 percent. The poverty rate for children whose better-educated parent had a high school degree was 29.2 percent; and with some college, it was 15.2 percent. Only 2.8 percent of children under 6 living in poverty had a parent with a college degree.

Education for women is especially important. In 1997, children under age 6 living with single mothers were five times as likely to be poor (56 percent) as were those living with both parents (11 percent). Out-of-wedlock births and a high divorce rate, combined with the lack of responsibility many men feel toward children they father, have created an environment where children suffer poverty. Even low-income married women who find themselves widowed will need a source of independent income— namely a job—as Social Security survivor and dependent benefits provide a minimum of support.

The need for education for women and girls in other countries is even more severe. While many girls are held back from school because of cultural restraints, many of the poorest have no access to a school—they live too far from a school, or there are not enough schools for all students. United Nations Educational, Scientific and Cultural Organization (UNESCO) estimates that 100 million children around the world have no access to schools. When only one child in a family can be sent to school, it is usually the oldest son.

HEALTH CARE

Poor women and children are also less likely to receive health care than affluent women and children, or poor men. Ironically, in the United States sometimes it is those who work the hardest who receive the least health care. They earn too much money to receive government health insurance, but earn too little to pay for their own private insurance. They work for little pay and no benefits, so health insurance from an employer is out of the question.

It was to help people like this that Mountain Hope Good Shepherd Clinic was begun in Sevier County, Tennessee. Thousands of people come to the area every year to enjoy the mountains, the skiing, and the tourist spots like Gatlinburg and Pigeon Forge. Many people also come because, as clinic physician Dr. Alyene Reese put it, "A lot of young people move to Sevier County thinking this is the pot of gold, but they don't know jobs are low paying with no benefits."

Reese retired in Sevier County after 35 years of medical practice in Tuscaloosa, Alabama. She went to work as a local school nurse, and what she saw among the school children motivated her to open a clinic for the working poor.

"When we started getting figures on people who didn't have health insurance, we found we needed a primary care clinic because there were more adults than kids without health insurance."

That is not to say the clinic does not see children. Many pediatric patients come in with colds, skin infections, vomiting, and diarrhea. Among adults, many have allergies, which the wet mountain weather aggravates; there is also a tremendous amount of substance abuse, ranging from cigarettes and alcohol to drug abuse. Many patients do hard manual labor and sustain back injuries, which can lead to addiction to prescription pain killers. Body piercings and tattoos can lead to hepatitis. There is also a high rate of type 2 diabetes, and malnutrition, American style.

"There's obesity because they get the wrong foods, the kind that are easier to get and easier to fix. They work like crazy but get little real exercise," Reese explained.

The clinic sees few people from Appalachia because state health care is available for them. But the people who do the hard work of keeping the resort areas running might work two or even three jobs and still not be able to afford health care, including dental and psychiatric care.

"People don't get dental care until things are so bad they need a tooth pulled." The burden of so much work for so little reward, combined with other stressors, also leads to much depression and substance abuse. A full-time counselor and counselor interns run a counseling clinic.

Although the fees for clinic services—which start at $5.50 for the first visit and $2.50 after that—are based on a sliding fee scale, if a person has no money at all, care is still provided. Currently, about 150 patients are seen each week, with Reese seeing the children.

"When we get a full-time doctor who can see adults, we can see more patients," she said.

Reese and her friend, social worker Sue Ellen Riddle, began the clinic, but by no means take the credit for either its funding or its success. Churches, individuals, city and county governments, and civic organizations like the Rotary Club fund the clinic. Many specialists will take referrals pro bono, and the clinic uses the free drug programs many pharmaceutical companies offer. Reese has noticed that people who have known some type of hardship themselves are the most likely to help those in need. For those who are not convinced that the patients couldn't pay their own way, Reese issues an invitation to come to the clinic.

"When they see our patients, learn how hard they work at jobs that nobody else wants, learn how many jobs some of them have, it changes their attitude." She warns everyone, however, against judging whether a patient is deserving of care.

"We are doing this work for God," she stated. While she sees the habits that cause some of her patients' problems, she understands that their overeating or drug use helps them temporarily forget about "the mess they are in." She also urges Christians not to look down on the poor or have the attitude, "Well, good me is going to help poor you." She points out that the poor are criticized for many of the same vices and behaviors the rich display, yet the rich do not receive a word of reproach.

The clinic staff prays with its patients, and has seen their habits and lives change. Ministry to a patient can affect an entire family, or the patient for a lifetime. One patient that stands out in Reese's mind is an 18-year-old boy who came in with his neck horribly swollen. Another doctor had diagnosed him simply with swollen lymph nodes. He had gone to a specialist who told him it would cost $8,000 just to get a diagnosis. The clinic staff immediately sent the boy for an x-ray.

"The radiologist called me and said his airway was almost completely closed and he'd be dead in three days if something wasn't done. It was obviously a malignancy. I'd never seen anyone with a neck that looked like that before," Reese recalled. She called an oncologist friend at Baptist Hospital in Knoxville.

"Bring him right over," the oncologist urged. The diagnosis was quickly made—Hodgkin's disease.

The boy is now in remission, but the story could have ended very tragically if not for the ministry of Mountain Hope Good Shepherd Clinic to the young and poor.

"He was just a boy," Reese recalled. "Just a young boy with his whole life ahead of him and parents who loved him."

PROJECT IDEAS

Almost every project idea listed in this book can also be used to minister to poor women and children. One of the most important ways to help these populations is through advocacy (see chap. 10). Other ideas are:

- Free or affordable childcare. This could be short-term, such as keeping a woman's children so she can go to the doctor, or ongoing care such as keeping children for women while they attend a literacy class. Afterschool care for working mothers is also a way to help women earn money for their families and form relationships with their children at the same time. If a fee must be charged, a sliding fee scale is usually helpful and fair.

- Adopt a women's shelter. Most shelters for battered women are in secluded places for the protection of the residents, but there are ways to help. Call the director or volunteer liaison and ask how your Woman's Missionary Union® (WMU®) group or church can support the shelter. Churches have provided meals, toiletries, cleaning supplies, and clothing for women, as well as school supplies and toys for their children. Ask about picking up residents for church services and children for Vacation Bible School and other church activities.

- Start or support a clinic for the poor, such as the one featured in this chapter.

- Start a mothers' meeting where women can learn parenting techniques, meal planning and budgeting, crafts, and have Bible study. This provides both spiritual and emotional nurture.

- Provide a counseling service through your church.

- Start a children's Bible club or day camp in a low-income area.

- Start a Christian Women's Job Corps® (CWJC℠) site.

PRAYER STRATEGY

Pray for women:
- Pray for strength and determination for women struggling to free themselves from welfare, or obtain a better job, through job training and mentoring programs such as CWJC or through literacy programs. Intercede for their physical and spiritual needs.
- Pray for hope and faith for women who are single heads of households, whether those households include young children, grown children who have returned home, or elderly parents. Pray that they will say, "As for me and my house, we will serve the Lord" (Josh. 24:15 NKJV).
- Ask God to protect women in war zones from torture, rape, and displacement from their homes. Pray that they would see God as their Rock and Protector.
- Pray for women who have been sold into slavery, that they would not give up in despair. Ask God to free their bodies and souls from bondage.
- Intercede for women trying to better themselves through owning farms, livestock, or small businesses. Pray that they will see God cares about their physical needs.
- Ask God to help battered women escape their abusers and find Christians who will help them start a new life.

Pray for children:
- Pray for children who are sick and have no hope of treatment. Ask God to heal their bodies and soothe their spirits with His love and presence.
- Intercede for children orphaned through war and diseases such as malaria and AIDS. Pray that they will learn God is their Provider and Protector.
- Pray for children sold into slavery. Ask God to deliver them from evil and help them to grow up mentally, physically, and spiritually free and strong.

- Ask God to help children in famine-stricken areas; pray that their bodies will not be permanently damaged, and that adults will care for them.
- Pray for children who want to go to school but cannot. Pray that God will move the hearts of their parents to allow their children as much education as is available to them.

Pray for Christians who can help:
- Ask God to burden the hearts of Christians with the reality of slavery. Pray that Christians with political power and freedom of speech will work to stop the trafficking in human beings.
- Pray God's blessings on missionaries and volunteers who bring education to women and children that otherwise would be neglected, who bring health care to families who otherwise would be left to suffer, and who bring food to those who are hungry and malnourished.
- Pray that Christians will understand the dynamics of domestic violence and will refuse to tolerate it.
- Ask God to move upon the hearts of Christians to give sacrificially to those who lack food, clothing, medicine, education, and the opportunity to hear the gospel.

4

POVERTY AND CULTURAL SENSITIVITY

"Accept one another then, just as Christ accepted you, in order to bring praise to God" (Rom. 15:7).

When the game called Ghettopoly hit the market, merchants claimed they couldn't keep the game on the shelves. Buyers in the US and Europe apparently couldn't wait to play the inner-city version of Monopoly. (Parker Brothers, the makers of the original Monopoly game, immediately threatened legal action for trademark infringement against the makers of Ghettopoly.)

Ghettopoly, like Monopoly, had players move their game piece across a board, gaining and losing money based on a combination of business acumen and luck. But instead of buying Park Place and utilities, players are in a culture of gangsta rap and get rich by running prostitution rings, robbing banks, and building crack houses. Not surprisingly, the game sparked a firestorm of controversy. The creator, David Chang, said the point of the game is satire, not glorification or humiliation of African-Americans. He asserted the game helped people laugh at themselves rather than live in "blame and bitterness."

The Reverend Robert P. Shine Sr., president of the Black Clergy of Philadelphia and Vicinity, saw it differently. He called the game "a corporate endorsement of the denigration of African Americans." He warned that if people did not speak out, there would be more to come. He predicted correctly because Chang said that based on the popularity of the game, he intended to bring out several other versions: Hoodopoly, Hiphopopoly, Thugopoly, and Redneckopoly.

The controversy over a board game can be seen as a microcosm of the greater conflict over cultural sensitivity today. What one group intends as harmless humor, another group finds offensive. Media developers could not understand why their idea for a reality TV show putting poor southern whites in affluent surroundings offended people in Appalachia. They argued, Wouldn't it be hilarious to watch such people learn to use indoor plumbing? No, said social workers and community developers from Kentucky and West Virginia, it would not be funny.

While educators and the media constantly press for both tolerance and diversity, it sometimes seems impossible to have it both ways. To try to view everyone as the same draws criticism that one's culture, race, or ethnicity is being ignored. To acknowledge differences runs the risk of appearing to stereotype or judge one group as better or worse than another.

Yet, cultural sensitivity is a prerequisite for Christians involved in ministry. And just to make it more interesting, in addition to being sensitive to different religious backgrounds, ethnicities, and cultures, anyone ministering among the poor must be culturally sensitive to economic class as well. This is true whether one is in the Rio Grande valley, inner-city Philadelphia, or rural Romania. Human beings are very good at finding differences in groups and devising reasons to look down on one group or another.

The gospel of Jesus Christ is the antidote to such conde-scension and scorn, for it teaches that Christ died for all and that in Him "there is neither Jew or Greek, . . . there is neither male or female; for you are all one in Christ Jesus" (Gal. 3:28 NKJV).

To be culturally sensitive to the poor, one must first realize that there are levels of rich and poor in the same geographic location, the same ethnic or racial group, and usually even within the same extended family. Each person carries attitudes about poverty. David Chang, the creator of Ghettopoly, found out that many African Americans who lived in the inner city found nothing humorous about crack addiction, prostitution, and gang warfare. They had lived among those evils and seen what destruction they caused. But also, many upper- and middle-class African Americans resented what seemed to be the assumption that all people of color came from a "gangsta-rap" culture. Just as different subgroups within the larger African American community had different reactions to the game, so will different members of any group react to any set of assumptions about them. This is true whether the assumptions come from a member of the group or an outsider, though assumptions from outsiders are often met with more hostility.

For example, the biggest shock many affluent Christians receive when they begin to minister to the poor is the discovery that *not everybody wants to be just like them.* Not everyone aspires to be upper class, or even middle class, and the poor recipients of well-intended ministry may not hesitate to tell their benefactors so.

Unwritten rules control any social class. To escape from poverty, the poor must be able to learn the rules of the affluent classes. Likewise, in order for teachers, social workers, and Christians to relate to the poor, they need to understand the unwritten rules of surviving poverty. Likewise, to escape from their poverty, the poor need to know the rules of upper- and middle-class people.

Ruby Payne, author of *A Framework for Understanding Poverty*, maintains that when poor do not know the unwritten rules for the upper classes, they are wrongly seen as being stupid or unteachable. As long as a "helper" tries to relate to the poor by talking down to them, there will be no real relationship built.

The belief that poor people are stupid, lazy, or uncaring is only one example of a damaging stereotype that keeps people apart. Another false belief is that a poverty characteristic is really a race characteristic. This is based on another stereotype, that all people of color are poor.

Payne recognizes that while wealthier people are respected for their competence, poor people respect strength. It is the only thing that keeps them from being victimized. This in part explains why violence is so often a part of life for the poor; physical strength has to be proven and dominance maintained in order to be secure. Strength in numbers is also crucial to survival.

The need for security can explain why so often, poorer people will show up for appointments, ranging from trial dates to doctor appointments, with a number of friends and family in tow. To those who don't know the unwritten rules of poverty, it may seem inappropriate or even silly for eight people to accompany one person to conduct business. Missing this social cue can affect everything that happens from then on.

For example, a Baptist center volunteer may get frustrated when a woman comes to apply for assistance and brings to her interview her husband, their small children, her mother, and her mother-in-law. The center waiting room is now completely taken over by this one family. Other clients have to stand up or wait outside. The volunteer is annoyed, especially when all the adults crowd into the interview area and leave the children unattended in the waiting room.

The volunteer is looking at the situation from the framework of the middle class. The adults are behaving inappropriately by all coming into a private interview. They are irresponsible for leaving the children to run wild. The young woman must not be smart enough to handle the interview by herself.

With more attention to the rules of poverty, the volunteer might see things differently. The family is there to support the young woman. The poor are used to getting "the runaround," so they have come to lend their strength. Perhaps the young woman has few reading and writing skills and another adult will need to fill out paperwork. Or, since poor families are often led by strong females, it's possible her mother and mother-in-law feel they are actually in charge of the family.

Paying attention to the rules of poverty does not mean the volunteer has to accept the situation. She could explain that the center does not provide childcare and children must not be left unattended. She could then ask the mother and mother-in-law to stay with the children while the husband remains with his wife. The volunteer could then begin to build a relationship with the couple, and their lives could be changed.

GIVING HOPE WHERE LIFE IS HARD

Relationship building is vital to sharing the gospel with the poor. Boyd Hatchel, an International Mission Board (IMB) missionary assigned to the Gypsy, or Romany, people of Romania, explains that being sensitive to their unique culture is a crucial part of building ministering relationships where one is allowed to share Christ.

"The Gypsies, also known as the Romany, are on the bottom rung of every ladder of every society. Yet where life is hardest, people are often most receptive to the gospel message. This has been true with the Gypsies."

Life has been hard for this people group, who, like the Jews, were a target of Nazi extermination during the Holocaust. Their lack of education and the persecution they have suffered continue to make life a struggle. According to the United Nations Educational, Scientific and Cultural Organization (UNESCO), more than 60 percent of Romania's Gypsies are believed to live below the poverty level; 80 percent have no formal educational qualifications to help them get a job. Their housing is substandard, and their life expectancy is less than 50 years.

Their poverty status is entwined with their high rates of illiteracy in both Romany, their heart language, and Romanian, the national language. For this reason, oral storytelling works much better than tracts or written Bible studies. Hatchel and his co-workers use chronological Bible storying with the Gypsies. The Gypsy people are very receptive to storying, but there are cultural issues that call for sensitivity on the part of the storyteller.

For example, because of the poverty and suffering Gypsies endure, they avoid health-and-wealth teachings that avoid sacrifice and glorify Western materialism.

A storyteller also needs to pay attention to cultural constraints. Hatchel would advise a volunteer working with the Gypsies to avoid US illustrations and fantasy. A woman would never share a story to a mixed group. A child's story would only be told to children.

Ministry as well as witness should be tailored to what the people group needs. Agricultural ministries are needed in a farming community; well-drilling would be a blessing in drought-prone areas. Not all poor people need the exact same thing. For example, any younger Gypsies see owning their own businesses as a way out of poverty and a way to gain respect among the majority Romanian population. Hatchel suggests churches could help with small business instruction, as well as traditional activities like children's Bible clubs, camps, or music events. Horse veterinary clinics are another need that Christian volunteers could fill, as well as medical and dental projects for the Gypsies themselves. Most of all, churches could pray for the Gypsies, especially those who do not know Christ.

PREPARING FOR MINISTRY

Since any ministry to the poor would require sensitivity and understanding to the culture of the poor, many of these ideas can be used when undertaking any other ministry, such as hunger or health projects.

- Conduct ministry/witness training that includes looking at one's attitudes about the poor. Use a resource such as the work of Ruby Payne.
- Actively guard against your own use of ethnic slurs or degrading references like "poor white trash" when speaking about the poor.
- Plan worship services or community functions which bring the poor and well-to-do together as equals.
- Guard against unscriptural teachings that equate being rich with being spiritually superior.
- Teach a Bible study on reconciliation/respect for others.
- Learn about other groups and cultures rather than relying on stereotypes.

CROSS-CULTURAL MINISTRY IDEAS

- Sponsor a refugee family.
- Partner with a language church or a congregation in a poor area.

- Adopt a people group that is economically deprived. Find out how to pray for the group. If a missionary is assigned to work with the group, find out projects your church could do.

PRAYER STRATEGY

For self:
- Pray for God to reveal any prejudices against the poor that hinder your ability to love them.
- Pray for God to reveal any attitudes you have about money that distance you from the poor.
- Pray for God to cleanse you of anything unpleasing or unchristlike that would hinder you from serving the poor.
- Pray for wisdom and sensitivity to better minister to the poor.
- Pray for a more Christlike spirit in order to see the poor as Christ sees them.
- Pray for more opportunities to minister to the poor in ways that will neither offend nor shame them.
- Pray for God to show you how to work for justice for the poor.

For others:
- Pray for missionaries, both international and domestic, who work with the poor. Ask God to bless them with wisdom, hope, and strength for the work.
- Pray for churches and organizations that are reaching beyond their comfort zones to minister to the poor or to those very different from themselves.
- Pray for poor Christians, that they would be faithful witnesses to others.
- Pray for the poor who do not know Christ to place their faith in Him rather than in wealth.

- Pray that more Christians will obey God's commands to help the poor.
- Pray for the poor to receive justice and fair treatment.

Praises to God:

Losing prejudices against the poor—especially prejudices you didn't even realize you had—can be painful. One way to learn to appreciate and respect people of other cultural groups, including the poor, is by praising God for them. The following praise suggestions come from WMU, SBC's, Project HELP: Cultural Diversity Resource Kit.

- Praise God for the wonderful variety of cultures that form a beautiful mosaic of humanity.
- Praise God for the opportunities you receive to share the gospel with people who are different from you.
- Praise God for the things poor and oppressed Christians of the world have to teach others about faithfulness.
- Praise God for removing prejudices and replacing them with love and understanding.
- Praise God for giving us the ministry of reconciliation spoken of in 2 Corinthians 5:18–19.
- Praise God that Christ makes no difference in male, female, rich, poor, black, or white, "for you are all one in Christ Jesus" (Gal. 3:28 NKJV).

5

POVERTY AND HUNGER

"Jesus called his disciples to him and said, 'I have compassion for these people; . . . I do not want to send them away hungry'" (Matt. 15:32 NIV).

Hunger is the most universal symptom of poverty. One can argue whether a person is truly poor if she can't afford a television, a car, or other perceived necessity of modern life. Only someone out of touch with reality would assert that a person who can't afford food wasn't poor.

Hunger shows itself in different ways depending upon the area of the world one is in. High-income countries are dealing with an epidemic of obesity due in part to the fact that cheap foods often are also foods highest in empty calories and refined carbohydrates. Fresh fruits and vegetables and lean cuts of meat are beyond the reach of most of the very poor, unless their food budget is subsidized with food stamps and vouchers.

It is hard to equate hunger with obesity, until one considers that in order to feel full, a poor person in a First-World country may fill up on day-old bread, macaroni, and cheap lunchmeat. Hunger pains are reduced, but the person can still suffer from malnutrition, as well as diabetes, gout, and heart disease.

Despite many Americans being overweight, there are still others who go to bed hungry or on the verge of hunger. According to the respected hunger advocacy group Bread for the World, the latest census figures showed that 33.6 million people, including nearly 13 million children, live in households that know hunger or the risk of hunger. That works out to one in ten households nationwide. In some households, family members frequently skip meals or fast for an entire day. Nine million people, including 3 million children, live in these homes. This is 3.3 percent of US households.

Hunger directly affects another ill of poverty: illiteracy. While parents are eager for children to attend school so they can receive a free hot lunch, one meal a day, or a meal with snacks, will not meet a child's nutritional needs. Preschoolers and school-aged children who suffer severe hunger have higher levels of chronic illness, anxiety, and depression, according to a study cited by Bread for the World. Illness and anxiety impact a child's ability to learn. Severe, chronic hunger can affect brain development in very young children, condemning them to live with less intelligence and learning ability than they would have had otherwise.

In this way, by robbing children of the ability to think and learn, hunger hurts all of society. It robs the world of all that those children would have done with the natural gifts which God gave them.

Both Christians and secular agencies have tried to help the hungry, but their efforts are not enough. In 2002, the US Conference of Mayors reported that requests for emergency food assistance went up an average of 19 percent. Of those asking for assistance, 48 percent had children, and 38 percent were employed adults. High housing costs, low-paying jobs, unemployment, and a poorly performing economy led the list of reasons for the increase in requests.

Still, hunger in the US is only the tip of the iceberg. More than 840 million people around the globe are malnourished. Of those, 799 million are from the developing world, and 153 million are under the age of five. These children are the first victims of hunger—6 million babies, toddlers, and preschoolers die every year from hunger and malnutrition. More than 2 million children annually develop severe vision problems due to a lack of vitamin A.

Death from malnutrition can come in the form of a virus or infection like measles, malaria, influenza, or typhus which cannot be fought off with a weakened immune system. Death from pure hunger is a slow, horrible process.

First, the body consumes stored fat for energy. Then, it begins to draw protein from muscles and vital organs. The organs begin to shrink, blood pressure is reduced, and the body's systems do not work as efficiently. As the body weakens, anemia develops. When this progresses, the heart and lungs begin to fail. Inner body temperature falls. The person is weak, cold, and racked with hunger pains. In a total fast, hunger pains gradually diminish for a while; but when the body receives a handful of food now and then, the stomach stays active.

As starvation continues, the skin hangs in folds and parts of the body—especially the abdomen—swell with fluid. Hair becomes brittle and dry. When normal body weight is reduced by 30 percent, the immune system can't protect the body and fungi, viruses, and bacteria attack the person. Gastroenteritis—inflammation of the digestive membranes—often sets in at this point. It is the number one global cause of death for infants and children.

A pregnant woman who starves can anticipate either a miscarriage, a stillbirth, or a living child with birth defects.

One of the more ghastly aspects of death by starvation is that the person's mind remains clear for some time. They know what is happening.

Finally, the major organs fail and the person dies, like a candle flame gradually sputtering out into darkness.

The tragedy of hunger is made worse by the fact that it is unnecessary. Every country in the world, according to the United Nations' Food and Agriculture Program, has the capacity to feed its population, but poverty, war, and bad government policies prevent countries from doing this. Agricultural missionaries and other Christians who minister to the poor try to alleviate hunger in ways ranging from giving emergency food rations to serving hot meals to teaching new farming techniques, as is being done by International Mission Board missionaries in the Philippines.

MAKING JESUS KNOWN IN WORD AND DEED

The purpose of the Mindanao Baptist Rural Life Center (MBRLC) is to help all people, especially hill farmers, experience the abundant life Jesus spoke of in John 10:10 NKJV), "'I have come that they might have life, and that they may have it more abundantly.'" The mission of the MBRLC is to share the good news of the abundant life in Jesus Christ through a holistic Christian lifestyle. This is summed up in the theme Making Jesus Known in Word and Deed.

The MBRLC targets a community for development and spends an average of three years there. The extension personnel then enter the community to help lead the people to identify their needs and help them figure out solutions for those needs. The extension personnel are trained in agriculture, health care, and community development. The agricultural training is geared to helping farmers get the most out of the hilly farmland in the area. While this is done, mothers and village health workers receive training in nutrition, gardening, sanitation, and primary health care. The first year is a time of beginning and learning needs. The second year is the time to really implement projects. The third year is a time of winding down their involvement and having the villagers continue with what they have learned. The village is able to use the training to improve both food production and overall health, explained missionary Steve Musen.

"The average Filipino farmer in rural Mindanao earns only about $150–$200 per year. His life is very difficult. He cannot provide an adequate diet for his family. He does not produce the food which his family needs because of a lack of know-how and also because of the problem of soil erosion on hilly lands," Musen stated.

"He lacks good seeds and breeding stock. His family is often in poor health because of poor nutrition, poor sanitation, unsafe drinking water, and general lack of knowledge about primary health care."

The MBRLC opened in 1971 with missionary Harold Watson. Since its birth, the ministry has coupled community development with a strong evangelistic purpose. The MBRLC wants people to understand that God loves them. The gospel is shared and believers are discipled. The families of these isolated villages are shown God's love through the work of the MBRLC, which keeps many projects going to help the Filipino farm families. Some of these projects include FAITH (Food Always in the Home) Gardening; SALT 1 (Sloping Agricultural Land Technology); SALT 2 (Simple Agro-Livestock Technology); SALT 3 (Sustainable Agroforest Land Technology); SALT 4 (Small

Agrofruit Livelihood Technology); seed production and plant propagation; natural farming—hog production; and poultry, small animals, and inland fish.

Not all Christians can conduct the far-reaching projects and programs of the MBRLC, but there are many things that every church or Christian group can do to minister to the hungry.

PROJECT IDEAS
Local projects

The number one food ministry project is undoubtedly collecting food for a food pantry or Baptist center. Missionaries and volunteers are happy to receive donations, but health regulations may not permit them to use all donations. Examples of food that should not be donated include foods and baby formula that have passed the expiration date, home canned foods, and foods that have been exposed to extremes of temperature. Food pantries also find it difficult to use large bulk purchases, such as 50-pound bags of flour. When such items are donated, someone must take the time to divide up the items into smaller, useable portions.

One of the most helpful things a church or group can do when collecting food is to publicize what kinds of food the pantry can best use. The basic list of food pantry staples includes dried beans, pasta, rice, flour, powdered or canned milk, peanut butter, canned tuna, oatmeal, and toiletries that food stamps won't buy, such as soap and toothpaste. Since some people who receive emergency food assistance do not have electricity, nonperishable items that require no cooking, such as peanut butter or canned fruit, are especially welcome. A food drive is not the time to clean out one's pantry at home and get rid of odd items, like that can of black olives that was never used.

A food collection should be just the starting point of ministry, however. In order to build relationships with people, Christians must do more than send food for someone else to distribute. Other local hunger projects could be:
- Teach nutrition and cooking classes to low-income heads of households.
- Take a woman shopping and show her how to get the most for her money.
- Teach someone how to make a budget.
- Teach gardening, including community and windowsill gardening.
- Teach gleaning from supermarkets, restaurants, and bakeries to benefit food banks.
- Pack sack lunches for a homeless shelter's ministry.
- Volunteer in a soup kitchen.
- Deliver meals to homebound people.
- Drive an elderly person to a senior citizen feeding center.
- Help a person apply for food stamps and other food programs.
- Start a food pantry or volunteer with an existing ministry.
- Become a disaster relief volunteer.
- Conduct Vacation Bible School or children's Bible clubs in low-income areas. Provide healthy snacks and drinks, like apples and milk, instead of cookies and punch. Ministering to children is a good way to learn of other needs of families in the area.
- Bring a meal to a shelter for battered women.

International project ideas
- Go as a missions volunteer to help a missionary do agricultural ministries: teaching farming techniques, veterinary clinics, etc.
- Take a missions team from your church on a volunteer trip to help a missionary with agricultural ministries.

- If you cannot go yourself, support someone else as a missions volunteer.
- Support programs that supply farmers with seed and breeding stock.
- Conduct a mission study on agricultural missions and hunger ministries.
- Keep a bank on your dining room table; encourage family members to drop in change all year long to donate to the Southern Baptist World Hunger Offering. This is a good way to teach children about giving to others.
- Observe World Hunger Day in your church.
- Sponsor a refugee family.

PRAYER STRATEGY
Pray for those who minister to the hungry and poor:
- Missionaries, both domestic and international, who work in hunger relief
- Agriculturalists working to develop more sustainable ways to grow food
- Relief workers in refugee camps and disaster sites
- Volunteers in soup kitchens, food pantries, and feeding programs
- Social workers and nutritionists who work in government programs with the poor
- Teachers who teach in low-income schools where students are hungry or malnourished
- Lawmakers who have the power to legislate over food and humanitarian aid programs
- Government leaders who control food distribution and prices in their countries

Pray for those who are hungry:
- People living in shelters for the homeless and abused
- Those living in poverty because of unemployment or low fixed incomes
- The elderly and homebound who cannot get to a grocery store without help
- Children who depend on others to provide for them
- Refugees and disaster victims
- People living in areas hit by famine, drought, war, and plague
- Farmers forced to use poor quality techniques and equipment

Pray for Christians:
- To have more concern for the hungry, and for that concern to translate into action
- To practice sacrificial giving to missions offerings and local hunger programs
- To begin new food ministries or volunteer at existing ministries
- To be burdened for the spiritual as well as physical salvation of the hungry and poor
- To be more grateful for the food they have and to recognize it as a blessing from God
- To become advocates for the hungry, the sick, and the powerless
- To become better stewards of the food resources God has given them

6

POVERTY, AIDS, AND OTHER CRITICAL HEALTH ISSUES

"We love because he first loved us" (1 John 4:19 NIV).

According to the United Nations Development Programme (UNDP), there are now 40 million people living with HIV, the human immunodeficiency virus that causes AIDS. About 95 percent of the infected live in developing countries. That means the great majority of the ill live where there is the least chance of affordable medical care. Of all new infections in 2001, 68 percent were in sub-Saharan Africa and 16 percent were in South and Southeast Asia. It also means that the disease spreads quickest among the poor, who are less likely to be educated about HIV/AIDS. (In Bangladesh and Nepal, less than one in three married women have even heard of AIDS.)

AIDS has cost the world a generation of young people who could have been working and caring for their families. Globally, 24.8 million people have died since the beginning of the epidemic in the early 1980s. Despite global education campaigns, the infection continues to spread. In 2001, 5 million people became newly infected with the virus. About 14,000 people become infected with HIV every day. More than half these people are between 15 and 24 years old. Of the 11.8 million of these young infected people, the majority (7.3 million) are female.

If these numbers weren't staggering enough, there are also 3 million children living with HIV/AIDS, and an incredible 14 million who have been orphaned by AIDS. The UNDP predicts that number will reach 40 million by 2010.

While poverty affects the spread of AIDS because the poor are more likely to be uneducated about the disease and less likely to receive medical care, AIDS also increases poverty. According to UNDP, the percentage of people living in poverty in Burkina Faso will increase from 45 percent to nearly 60 percent by 2010 as a result of HIV/AIDS. In Zambia, in two-thirds of the urban households where the main wage earner died of AIDS, income dropped by 80 percent. Of these households, 61 percent had to move to find a cheaper place to live; 39 percent lost their running water.

Education is also hurt. In the Zambian study just mentioned, it was found that in these AIDS-affected households, 21 percent of girls and 17 percent of boys were forced to quit school. Not only are children deprived of schooling, the schools are deprived of teachers. According to UNDP: "In 1999, UNICEF estimated that 860,000 children in sub-Saharan Africa have lost their teachers to AIDS since the beginning of the epidemic."

Food production also declines in heavily infected countries. In the 27 most-affected African countries, 7 million agricultural workers have died from AIDS.

Healthy people are also kept away from work because of AIDS. It is possible in some parts of the world to attend a funeral every day for a neighbor or relative who has died of AIDS. In many cultures, it is necessary to attend a funeral, no matter what other obligations one has, including work. In sub-Saharan Africa, older people have often taken to attending funerals as the representatives of the younger family members, so the healthy relatives can continue working.

So many of the statistics dealing with HIV/AIDS infection come from Africa because it ranks number one among the continents for infection rates, though all the continents except for Antarctica have reported the disease. The rates in Africa, however, are many times what the rates are for areas such as western Europe and North America. Seventy percent of all HIV-infected adults live in Africa. That continent is a magnified example of what HIV/AIDS does to communities, families, and individuals.

Aren't the new blends of drugs—antiretrovirals—supposed to greatly improve an infected person's quality and length of life? Yes, but only 760,000 of the millions of HIV sufferers have access to these drugs, and most of them live in high-income countries. Of course, just living in a high-income country does not mean the person will be able to afford the medicines. In the United States, the triple cocktail of HIV drugs can cost between $10,000 and $12,000 a year.

HIV/AIDS is not the only global health threat. There are malaria, typhoid, cholera, influenza, Ebola, as well as new sicknesses like SARS. The diseases that kill the most people are not always the ones that get the most attention from the medical research community. For example, in 1998 spending on health research was about $70 billion. How much of this was spent on AIDS vaccine research? $300 million. And for malaria research, $100 million was spent.

Many global health threats are directly related to sanitation and nutrition. Even in areas that normally have good sanitation, a natural disaster such as a flood or earthquake can trigger the spread of typhoid and cholera. When thousands of people or animals are killed at one time, the bodies cannot all be buried in time to prevent disease. When floodwaters run through an area, private wells and public water systems are contaminated. Dirty water contributes to millions of deaths every year because of its ability to carry everything from parasites to dysentery germs to dead animal carcasses.

What are Christians doing in the face of such overwhelming need?

CHANGING HEARTS OF STONE

Missionaries Sharon and Larry Pumpelly have seen firsthand the misery created by AIDS in Africa. Not only are the young workers sickening, the deaths of the younger generation leave older Africans without the support of their grown children—the only kind of social security they had. Now these elderly people are faced with supporting themselves and their orphaned grandchildren.

While AIDS leads to increased poverty, the reverse is also true. The only hope most Africans have is through education. Most young Africans don't have the money even to finish grade school, much less go on to high school and college. They require a patron who will buy the books, pay the fees, etc. Many of these patrons expect sexual favors in return, but these patrons are not the only ones who want sex as payment for services.

"Those without are often at the mercy of those who have, even if what they have is a simple service. Truck drivers, schoolteachers, bosses, and others will exploit sexually those who need their services just to survive or to have a hope out of poverty," says Sharon.

In such an environment, HIV can and does spread quickly. The key to better treatment is early detection, but

AIDS carries a great stigma in Africa, and people do not want to be tested. "The financial cost to being tested is low, but the emotional cost is very high," Sharon explains. Missionaries have been encouraging pastors to be tested with their wives and deacons in order to reduce the stigma associated with testing. This is important even in churches, for many first-generation Christians have already been infected before coming to know the Lord.

The attitude of Christians toward those infected is also crucial to any effective ministry. In 2001, the Pumpellys held a conference with Baptist leaders of Kenya and Tanzania. The conference covered topics such as praying for those affected by AIDS, counseling, support groups, True Love Waits, and related issues. Sharon quickly realized that some people had come with the assumption that they were offering projects with funding. One woman stated that she had come reluctantly and intended to leave quickly if she did not find the conference useful.

The conference was in two phases. At the end of phase one, Sharon guided participants to begin filling out an evaluation form. She asked for someone to respond to the question, What have you gained by being at this conference? People began to weep. The woman who had earlier threatened to leave told the audience that her son had died of AIDS, yet she had still believed everyone who died of AIDS deserved it. After what she had seen and heard in the conference, she was led to repent of those thoughts and feelings. (That woman now is a volunteer training other women in AIDS ministry.)

The next person to speak was a pastor who said that he planned to stop at the hospital on his way home from the conference to repent to someone there. He also planned to volunteer as a chaplain at the hospital so he could minister to anyone—no matter what problem they were facing.

"I honestly felt like the most blessed missionary in the whole world because God allowed me to see His hand in changing hearts of stone to hearts of flesh," Sharon said.

Since that conference the Baptist Convention of Kenya has begun the Baptist AIDS Response Agency (BARA), with trainers traveling all over Kenya training churches in a response to AIDS. They are opening voluntary counseling and testing centers in churches. The youth branch of BARA is training young people in the African version of True Love Waits, and True Love Waits clubs are springing up. BARA is also developing a program for married couples called True Love Stays.

"Our hope is that lives will be changed—some for pure healthy living; some to die with hope; and that nations will be changed as the individuals within them embrace Christ and honor Him in their lives," says Sharon.

PROJECT IDEAS

Whole books have been devoted to ministering to people with AIDS or other life-threatening illnesses in one's local community, so only a few ideas will be touched on here. Other project ideas will address how to minister to the global health crisis through assisting international missionaries.

Local ideas

- Form care teams. Members will take turns helping the sick person or family members with transportation, childcare, respite care, spiritual nurture, meals, or other daily chores, from bathing the dog to adjusting the TV antenna.
- Become a hospice volunteer. Hospice programs assist the terminally ill to die with as much peace and dignity as possible, while offering support to the patient and family

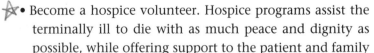

members. Hospice programs offer training to volunteers. There are also special projects throughout the year in which church groups can donate time or resources.

- Have a health-care worker appreciation day. Conduct a special service in your church or your community to say thank you to health-care workers who sacrifice so much to care for the sick.
- Contact the community health program or local AIDS clinic and ask for a list of toiletries and other items that you can donate.
- Become an advocate with insurance companies, government agencies, and hospitals. Help with filling out paperwork. Never offer medical or legal advice yourself; help them find professionals for these services.
- Offer to take the sick person, or their family members, to church.
- Promote True Love Waits in your church and community.
- Support local efforts to teach health education, including nutrition, childcare, stop smoking campaigns, antidrug efforts, and home safety. Your county agricultural extension system is a key resource in this area.
- Become an advocate to communities with no clean water. Even in the United States, there are communities where people have to choose between washing their clothes or flushing their toilets because of lack of water. They must buy bottled water for cooking and drinking because no public water system exists in their area or they are too poor to hook onto an existing system.
- Join a disaster relief team. Part of such a team's purpose is to help provide clean water and food in areas hit by floods, storms, or earthquakes.
- Promote N'tl AIDS Awareness Day in November.
- Promote World AIDS Day (Dec. 1)

International ideas
- Learn about AIDS in Africa and around the world. Order the AIDS prayer guide and video from the International Mission Board (IMB) (see resources).
- Contact regions through the IMB to learn of various projects concerning AIDS which are happening in the different regions. There are AIDS-related ministries outside of Africa, too.
- Volunteer to go with a medical or dental team missions group. Many missionaries need volunteers to do clinics in remote or impoverished areas. If you can't go personally, ask how you can support the team.
- Be an advocate for more medical research targeting infectious diseases; for clean water and sanitation for all people; for health education and preventive health care.

PRAYER STRATEGY

Pray for the AIDS epidemic in Africa.
Sharon Pumpelly has provided the following list of prayer requests to include in a prayer strategy that is AIDS-specific.
- Pray for True Love Waits ministries in Africa and the rest of the world.
- Pray for HIV (He Is Victorious) projects and teams in Southern Africa.
- Pray for the Baptist AIDS Response Agency in Kenya.
- Pray for self-help groups in many of the sub-Saharan African countries, targeting widows, orphans, and families affected by AIDS.
- Pray for the hope of Christ to penetrate hearts and minds.
- Pray for the stigma of AIDS in the church to be changed to compassion and ministry.

Pray for the AIDS epidemic in the United States and around the world.

The following prayer requests were first offered through Project HELP: AIDS.

- Pray for pastoral counselors and chaplains ministering to people with AIDS.
- Pray for a cure for the disease.
- Pray for better and more affordable drugs to reach the people in need.
- Pray for medical personnel—doctors, nurses, technicians, nursing assistants, paramedics—who risk infection in order to care for those with HIV/AIDS.
- Pray for public health workers attempting to educate people about HIV/AIDS.
- Pray for the families and caregivers who daily take on the duties of caring for those with AIDS.
- Pray that people at risk will have the courage to be tested early.

7

POVERTY AND ILLITERACY

"Endeavor to see the needs of the world from God's stand-point." Fannie E. S. Heck

The world's poorest people are also the most illiterate, and the most illiterate are likely to be the poorest. Poverty and illiteracy are two hands that together put a chokehold on a person's hopes of a better life. Most of these people are women.

According to the United Nations Educational, Scientific and Cultural Organization (UNESCO), illiteracy rates for females are higher than those for males in every major area of the world: developed countries, Latin America/Caribbean, East Asia/Oceania, sub-Saharan Africa, the Arab states, and South Asia. But while the illiteracy rates in the so-called developed world are low and almost even, the rates in other areas are greatly uneven. For example, in the Arab states, the illiteracy rate for men is about 29 percent. For women, it's well over 50 percent. In South Asia the ratio of male-to-female illiteracy is about the same as in the Arab states, but the overall rates are higher—almost 60 percent for females.

According to the National Literacy Act of 1991, literacy is an "individual's ability to read, write, and speak in English and compute and solve problems at levels of proficiency necessary to function on the job and in society, to achieve one's goals, and develop one's knowledge and potential." While this is a definition for the United States, *English* could be substituted for any language used as the "gateway" to a culture. In countries where newspapers, job applications, and other important documents are written in Spanish, Arabic, Chinese, or some other language, the inability to read and write is just as crippling, if not more so, than it is for native English speakers in the US.

In countries with high levels of immigration, such as the US and Canada, literacy includes the needs of English as a second language (ESL). A person may be highly literate in her native language, but speak only broken English. That person has a literacy need. And for the millions who cannot read or write their native tongue, learning to read and write a second language is exceedingly difficult because they do not have the experience of learning those skills in their first language. The groundwork for literacy has not been laid.

Illiteracy is not just a Third-World problem. The United States, for all its emphasis on education, has millions of citizens whose native language is English, yet who cannot read or write at a functional level. This problem is creating another problem, poverty. In 1996 the National Survey of American Families (NSAF) surveyed heads of households. They found that 35.2 percent of low-income heads of households had less than a GED or high school diploma. Only 4.3 percent of higher-income families had a head of household without a high school education. When the NSAF figured in heads of households with only a high school diploma or GED, another 39.3 percent were low income. This mean 74.5 percent of all low-income families had a head of household with at best a high school diploma or GED. According to literacy consultants for the North American Mission Board, a typical illiterate American is male, under age 40, and has graduated from high school. So even those low-income heads of household—male or female—who hold a high school diploma very often cannot read or write at a working level.

Illiterate people, whether native English speakers or immigrants, are more likely to be cheated and taken advantage of than people who are literate. They have much less chance of getting a decent job, of knowing their legal rights, and of knowing how to go about finding help when they need it. When they are cheated, it is easier to confuse them and convince them that they are the ones who are wrong. *? not necessarily, street smarts!*

It should be said that not all illiterate people are poor. Some very hardworking, talented individuals have been able to rise in their professions—even graduate college—without being able to read or write. Many more, however, have had to refuse better jobs or more responsibility because they knew they couldn't do the reading and writing required. "I had to say, 'No, I don't really want to better myself,'" one nonfunctional reader said bitterly when he had to turn down a promotion.

Even the ones who do succeed financially carry a heavy burden of anxiety and shame that someone will find out their secret. They also still live without many benefits that literate people enjoy: they cannot read some street signs, they can never enjoy a book or magazine unless it is on tape, and they can't read notes from their child's teacher. As one mother from rural Kentucky said wistfully, "It would mean the world to me if I could just read my child a bedtime story."

Illiteracy hurts, and it hurts more than just the person who can't read or write. Their families are hurt because they are less likely to enjoy many of the benefits of life and more likely to endure poverty. In some cases, the illiteracy of the parent can lead to an imbalance in the entire family. This is especially true for immigrant families when the children pick up English at school and the parents still cannot speak or read the language.

Such a situation often arises among refugees, according to Richard Robinson, area manager for refugee resettlement with Lutheran Family Services in the Carolinas. "The refugees often come from societies where the parents were definitely the authority figures. Then they come to this country and the children learn to speak English and learn the culture faster than the parents. The parents become dependent on the children, who now hold all the power and sometimes use that fact against their parents. It's humiliating and frustrating for the parents."

When families hurt because of illiteracy, the community suffers. Society at large hurts because the person cannot contribute to the economy, and because illiteracy is a contributing factor to the crime rate. Of the general prison population, in the 1990s, 60 percent of the prison population and 85 percent of all juvenile offenders were functionally illiterate. Lack of reading skills hurts the health of a nation when people can't read the directions on medicine bottles or tell the doctor their symptoms.

Finally, illiteracy hurts the work of the gospel because people cannot read the Bible and learn about God's love for them and God's desire for them to repent and believe.

What about the functional illiterate?

STORYING THE BIBLE WITH THE ASHÉNINKA

Missionaries and local churches can't wait until a people group all become literate before sharing the gospel. Literacy ministries sometimes progress very slowly. A method of sharing the Scripture with nonliterate societies has been

developed. It's called chronological Bible
Since many poor people groups have n
their history, genealogy, songs, and t
become masters at the art of oral communica
type of oral communication.

Marty and Dena McAnally, missionaries with the International Mission Board (IMB), use CBS with the Ashéninka people of Peru. They train Christian leaders in the method, and they do some storying to large groups. Their goal, however, is to have Ashéninka men do the storying as much as possible, so that it will be an indigenous work—coming from the Ashéninka themselves rather than from outsiders.

"We have found CBS to be a good tool for this largely illiterate society and they enjoy hearing the stories," Marty said. "Understanding of the Scriptures comes more rapidly. Traditional analysis of verses out of context has often left people confused.

"Christian leaders trying to teach without any training or Bible knowledge have left the impression that the Bible is only about a very limited set of do's and don'ts. We have found that when the Scriptures are clearly presented through storying and the opportunity to accept Christ as Savior is given, many people are ready to respond."

Storying among the Ashéninka can lay the groundwork for church planting. In a community called San Pedro, there were a few believers who needed a teacher. One of the Ashéninka church planters was related to this group, and he went with the missionaries to do storying and disciple believers. A number of new converts were made, and the church planter baptized several, including his own brother, on his next visit. His newly baptized brother is now the pastor for this group of believers. They are continuing to see the gospel spread among this community.

The Ashéninka are a very poor people in the physical sense. They live in central and eastern Peru along a number of rivers and scattered across thousands of square miles of jungle. As subsistence farmers, they carve out small fields from the jungle. Their houses are on raised platforms, with no walls to keep out the wind and rain. Their protein comes mainly from fish and wild birds and pigs which they hunt. This game is more scarce than one might think, and the Ashéninka suffer from malnutrition and parasites.

The hard life takes a toll quickly. "Very old people are uncommon," Marty said. In addition to their illiteracy and poverty, the Ashéninka suffer from prejudice from Peruvians of mixed Spanish Indian ancestry. Most look down on them or ignore them, and they can expect little help.

The McAnallys have found through their work with the Ashéninka that helping the poor has its own hazards. Just by giving things to some of the people, they have hurt the testimony and reputation of the Ashéninka Christians.

"The grapevines in the Ashéninka world are very active and tend to produce false information," Marty said. "We have learned through mistakes to be careful." The people do ask for things, and the McAnallys want to help, but they try to avoid making the people dependent on them.

"We want them to stand on their own feet so that when we leave nothing will have to change. They truly like to receive from us and we love to give. We have to do it prayerfully and carefully."

While they do not ask churches to help with most physical ministries, the McAnallys welcome medical teams and hold clinics whenever they have volunteers.

PROJECT IDEAS

Because there are three branches of literacy ministries—adult reading and writing for native English speakers, ESL, and tutoring children and youth—there are dozens and dozens of ways to minister. The best way to begin is probably to select one type of literacy and focus on it at first. If there is not already such a ministry in your area, ask your state convention's literacy consultant to come and speak with your association, church, or WMU organization about the types of literacy ministries and the training involved in each. The North American Mission Board, working with state conventions, have trainers to teach 16-hour programs to equip volunteers in the three ministry areas.

There are many other way to minister through literacy besides being a volunteer.

- Participate in a community assessment survey of literacy needs.
- Provide childcare for adults in literacy classes.
- Sponsor a graduation ceremony for students who complete either an adult literacy or GED class.
- Help pay for books and materials for a literacy student.
- Mentor a woman with poor reading skills in Christian Women's Job Corps.
- Provide transportation for a literacy student to and from class.
- Offer citizenship classes for internationals.
- Drive a mobile library van.
- Teach someone to use a computer.
- Collect books and school supplies for a local school.
- Provide school fees and supplies for a needy student.
- Take an international woman grocery shopping. Show her how to read sale notices and use coupons.
- Teach a person how to make change and use a bank's services.

- Host special church services and parties for internationals in your community.
- Provide *Contemporary English Version* Bibles for literacy ministries. This is a Bible written in simple, modern English that low-level readers can understand.
- Become an advocate for literacy on the local, state, and national levels.
- Have a literacy awareness service at your church. Include appreciation for teachers in addition to publicizing literacy needs. Ask someone to share his or her testimony about what being able to read the Bible means to him or her.
- Go as a missions volunteer on either a North American or international missions trip and help with literacy programs.
- Provide the Bible on tape for someone who cannot read.
- Provide the Bible or Scripture portions in an international person's native language.

PRAYER STRATEGY

Pray for those teaching literacy:
- All teachers, whether at public or private schools, homeschoolers, or missionary moms teaching their children at home
- Missionaries involved in literacy ministries
- Missionaries who use chronological Bible storying
- Volunteers in ESL, adult reading and writing, and tutoring children and youth ministries
- Churches sponsoring literacy ministries and afterschool programs
- Christian Women's Job Corps mentors helping clients with reading skills

- Secular agencies that promote reading and writing skills, such as job training centers and GED classes
- Those teaching prison inmates in both literacy and job skills

Pray for those who need help:
- Refugees and immigrants who cannot speak the language of their host country
- Wives of international students and businessmen who want an American friend to teach them American customs and speech
- Prison inmates
- Those who are desperately trying to hide the fact they cannot read
- Schoolchildren struggling to learn without physical and emotional resources
- Children taken out of school to work to support their families
- Girls living in cultures that do not value education for women
- Adults with learning disabilities who dropped out of school in discouragement
- Parents who can't read themselves and are trying desperately to help their children do better
- Those who hunger to read the Bible but cannot

Places to prayerwalk for literacy:
- Schools
- Libraries
- Prisons/juvenile detention centers
- Unemployment offices
- Homeless shelters
- Day cares/nursery schools
- Baptist centers

8

POVERTY, VIOLENCE, AND CRIME

"And what does the Lord require of you? To act justly and to love mercy and to walk humbly with your God" (Mic. 6:8 NIV).

A widely held stereotype of poor people is that they are all violent. This is based on the fact that crime rates are higher in poor neighborhoods, and many prison inmates are from low-income backgrounds. But the poor are not always the ones who commit violence. They are also the victims of violence. People living in poorly maintained, crowded conditions are easily victimized. Poverty drives some people to commit property crimes to support their needs; while in others, the stresses of poverty can lead to a breakdown in moral values and common respect for the rights of others. As one thief stated, "Nobody cares about me, so why should I care about anybody else? You look after Number One."

Poor people also find it more difficult to escape violent relationships. They lack the power and the resources to do so. They may also have never known anything different.

Nowhere is this more obvious than in the lives of low-income battered women. According to a paper written by Eleanor Lyon, a researcher mentioned, studies have shown that well over half of women receiving welfare have endured physical abuse from a male partner. Most also reported childhood physical or sexual abuse.

Income also affects a woman's plans to leave a violent relationship. A study of 800 women using Texas battered women's shelters showed that access to money, childcare, and transportation were key factors in their plans to leave their batterer for good. Only 16 percent of women with their own money planned to go back to their abuser.

While poverty leads to violence, the reverse is also true. Almost all prison inmates are men. When they are taken from the home, the wife is left to provide for herself and her children. When it is known the father is in prison, she is less likely to receive sympathy and help.

Children whose mothers go to prison are also more likely to be poor. In recent years the female prison population has increased. According to the National Institute for Literacy, by the end of 2000, there were 91,612 women in state or federal prisons. This was 6.6 percent of all prison inmates. In 2000, 22 percent of adult probationers and 12 percent of parolees were women. Most of the mothers who go to prison had legal custody of minor children. Someone else must care for those children when the mother is gone. The number of children with a mother in prison rose a staggering 98 percent from 1991 to 1999, while the number of children with a father in prison grew by 58 percent during the same time period. In 1992, 22 percent of all minor children with an incarcerated parent were younger than five. Most were less than ten years old, with the average age being eight. Studies show these children are at more risk to drop out of school, use drugs, and become victims of crime or offenders themselves.

Victims of violence also suffer. When a breadwinner is murdered, a fund may be set up to pay for funeral costs or college for the children, but the day-to-day cost of living for the survivors is not considered. Poorer people are less likely to have adequate life insurance, so their families will be left with even less than a middle-class victim's family. When victims are permanently injured or traumatized so badly as to be unable to cope, who is going to provide for them? Government assistance, if it exists, is in most cases not enough. Many people assume there is some agency "out there" somewhere which pays for medical care and counseling for victims. In some cases, a victim may receive restitution from the offender, but there is no assurance that will happen. And who can make adequate restitution for the loss of a breadwinner or the parent who cared for small children? Who will help care for the elderly parent whose adult child was taken from them?

Christians can make a difference in the lives of people touched by violence and crime, but they must do so with wisdom and sensitivity. Carla Hammonds, author of *Restorative Justice Ministry Resource Guide* makes the case that Christians must be careful to avoid doing more harm than good when venturing into this area. If Christians ignore the needs of offenders and their families, they will be accused—and rightly so—of deciding who is deserving of God's grace, of being judgmental. If Christians rush to publicly comfort the offenders and urge forgiveness before the victims have even begun to recover, they are seen as condoning the offender's actions and trying to "get them off." They are perceived as caring more about the offender than the innocent victim.

Christians can minister to everyone affected by violence, but the same people should not try to minister to both offender and victim. There are actually four groups

who need ministry in the aftermath of violence. Each has distinct needs. They are:
- Offenders
- Victims and their families
- Families of offenders
- Law enforcement/criminal justice professionals

Ministry to everyone involved should be based on the concept of restorative justice. Restorative justice educates and equips God's people to meet the needs of victims, offenders, law enforcement, and communities, resulting in biblical change in the criminal justice system. Its goal is to restore a sense of peace, or *shalom.*

Hammonds stated, "This can only happen when God's people get involved in bringing Christ to those hurt by the evil of crime."

BRINGING CHRIST TO OFFENDERS' FAMILIES

Many Christians find it easier to minister to the children of inmates than the inmates themselves. While ministry should be based on obedience to Christ's commands rather than what is easy, helping the children of inmates is a legitimate ministry and can be a good starting point for restorative justice ministries.

The following ministry ideas come from *Restorative Justice Ministry Resource Guide.*
- Invite families to church services and events. Offer to pick them up, and then spend time with them; don't leave them to fend for themselves.
- Establish a volunteer visitor center or hospitality house close to a prison. Provide family members with a quiet, comfortable place to wait while visiting their loved one. Stock it with refreshments and toys for children. Provide childcare if possible.

- Offer church space for a support group.
- Provide transportation so families can visit the offender.
- Pay for an inmate's child to go to camp, such as a Girls in Action® (GA®) or church summer camp.
- Help children write to their parents.
- Offer acceptance and love. Remember, they are not the ones who committed the crime.

MINISTERING TO OFFENDERS

Ministry projects with offenders who are in prison or jail must follow the strict guidelines laid down by the correctional facility. This is a nonnegotiable fact. Chaplains or other staff can help churches know what projects are and are not practical. Some popular suggestions are:

- Provide Christian literature and videos.
- Plan and lead worship services.
- Furnish greeting cards.
- Teach literacy classes, Bible studies, skills classes, parenting courses, and marriage enrichment seminars.
- Provide special ministries and services at holidays.
- Set up and maintain a lending library.

Ex-offenders especially need help. Ministry when a person is released from confinement can make the difference between leading a productive life and going back to jail. Ministry ideas for ex-offenders are:

- Help them find a job and place to live.
- Invite them to church.
- Lead a Bible study.
- Start an accountability team to help encourage and pray for the ex-offender.
- Teach them things they will need to know on "the outside." Modern culture changes very quickly. Some inmates have been in prison so long they may not be

familiar with some of the newer technological advances or expectations of society. (One female inmate was amazed when she saw a microwave oven for the first time. She also did not know how to use an ATM.)

In South Carolina, Screven Baptist Association found a way to minister to both inmates and their children. The association has 58 churches and 21,000 members. The association's churches donated more than 700 Christmas gifts for the children of inmates at MacDougall Correctional Facility. Volunteers took the gifts to the facility and inmates selected one toy per child. Volunteers then wrapped the gifts and addressed them for mailing. The presents were shipped in time for children to get them for Christmas. More than 150 inmates benefited from this Christian ministry.

Some people might argue that offenders do not deserve such ministry. Ask yourself who benefits from offenders committing new crimes, especially crimes of violence. Neither the victims, the offenders, the families, or society as a whole is better off when offenders are not helped to become law-abiding members of society.

MINISTRY TO VICTIMS AND THEIR FAMILIES

Victims and their families have already been hurt once. They do not need to be hurt again with insinuations that they are somehow to blame, lectures about forgiving the offender, and curious questions. They need patience, kindness, and understanding. They need to be able to express their doubt, fear, and anger, if they wish to do so. Listening, sitting with them during court proceedings, going with them to lawyer or doctor appointments—all of these are valid ministries. Other suggestions are:

• Repair property damage and make the home more secure. Hammonds suggests, "Something as simple as installing a dead-bolt lock or peephole may bring a sense of security a person needs. Repairing windows and doors immediately after the crime can be vital to their healing process."

- Begin a support group.
- Pray with the victim and family.
- Provide food, childcare, and other assistance to family while they attend legal proceedings.
- Do things to give the victim back a sense of control. Do not make decisions for them; ask them what they want.
- Find financial resources for the victim, or the family left without a breadwinner. Be an advocate for them.
- Don't forget about them. When a crime drops off the front page or off the evening news, it is still very fresh in the minds of the injured. Be a long-term minister.

MINISTERING TO LAW ENFORCEMENT/ CRIMINAL JUSTICE PROFESSIONALS

This is often the forgotten group when it comes to ministering to those touched by violence. Just because they have chosen this as a profession does not mean they are not emotionally and spiritually affected by what they see every day. Sometimes they become victims themselves, such as when an officer is killed or wounded in the line of duty. You can minister to them by:

- Having a service of appreciation for them. National Police Week is usually the third week of May. Recognize all law enforcement—police, deputies, game wardens, marine police, etc. Tie blue ribbons in prominent places as reminders to pray for them.
- Writing notes of appreciation/encouragement.
- Letting them know you are praying for them. Ask them for specific prayer requests.
- Sponsoring volunteer chaplains.

- Sending refreshments for the officers at their stations, the prison, or jail. Include every shift.
- Leading the children of your church to write notes thanking law enforcement for protecting their community.

PRAYER STRATEGY

When praying for victims and their families, ask for:

- Peace and security, especially the peace and security found in Jesus Christ
- Physical, emotional, and spiritual healing
- Strength, faith, and hope
- Understanding and help from people around them
- Justice and, if possible, restitution
- The physical resources they need

When praying for the families of offenders, ask:

- That their children be protected from evil influences
- That churches open their doors and hearts to them
- That the peace of Christ will enter their lives and ease the anxiety and shame they feel
- For the means to visit the offender
- For family ties to strengthen
- For Christians who will befriend them

When praying for offenders, ask for:

- Godly people in positions of authority in the correctional system
- Help for those overcoming addictions
- Protection for those who may be preyed upon by other inmates
- Healing for those who are sick in mind and body
- Christian volunteers and chaplains
- Their hearts to become receptive to the message of Christ

When praying for law enforcement/criminal justice professionals, ask for:

- Protection from despair, cynicism, and paranoia
- Physical safety and strength
- Their faith to find a resting place in Christ
- Openness in working with Christians who want to bring God's grace to the criminal justice system
- Good family relationships and a strong support network

9

ASSESSING NEEDS IN YOUR COMMUNITY

In chapter 2 we discussed the fact that poverty can be hidden in even the most affluent area, as in the story of the young house-sitter who couldn't buy food for herself and her child. She had to ask for help. If Christians wish to break the cycle of poverty, however, we can't wait for the poor to find us. We must find them. One way to do this is through a needs assessment.

A needs assessment does several things. It helps locate the poor and determines what needs they have, whether those needs are food or shelter, housing or employment, medicines or decent childcare.

A needs assessment also helps make Christians aware of the real situation. After a needs assessment, it becomes harder to hide behind generalities and stereotypes. It becomes harder to say, "People around here don't have those problems."

Finally, a needs assessment helps determine what is already being done. In her book on child advocacy *Precious in His Sight* Diana Garland writes that much good is being done, but often others don't know about it. The help doesn't reach all that it could, or the same help is offered by several other groups. Such duplication is inefficient. A needs assessment can lead to good networking with others who care about the poor.

WHAT EXACTLY IS A NEEDS ASSESSMENT?

A needs assessment is a time of fact-gathering by Christians for the purpose of designing and strengthening ministries that meet the needs of the community. A group will plan a tour of area agencies or professionals, then make appointments to go there. When there, the group will ask questions and gather data. The group will have a leader, and will begin and end each interview promptly. If there are many places to survey, several groups could divide up the sites. During the interviews the group should be careful not to make promises about help or even leave the impression that they will do certain things for the agency. Spend time listening to the agency representative rather than talking about what your church dreams of doing. All requests should be looked at during the debriefing sessions and ministry planning sessions later.

After finishing the interviews, the group will meet to share information and discuss how to best present what they have learned to the church or association.

WHO WILL DO THE ASSESSMENT?

One person can't do a complete needs assessment. For one thing, it would take too much time. For another thing, you would not be much better off because you would have one person trying to convince a lot of other people of what she has learned. The voice of several witnesses bears more weight than the voice of a single witness.

A group conducts a needs assessment, which is part survey, part interview. The assessment group should be made up of people who feel a burden for the needs of the poor, and who can express to others the information they gather. Some of the possible group members include pastor, director of missions, minister of missions, minister to children or families, WMU leader, men's ministry leader, women's ministry leader, deacons, volunteer coordinators of existing ministries, and concerned church members. College-aged people can participate, but this is not a task for children or youth. They can hear the report, but group members need to have a maturity level to be able to ask pertinent questions and gather information. There needs to be a balance between women and men, leaders and followers in this group. Different people will use their backgrounds to "hook" onto different insights and facts.

WHO DO WE ASSESS?

Several weeks before actually doing the assessment, decide what agencies or people you will interview. Here are some suggestions, but they are only suggestions. Your assessment will depend partly upon whether you are in an urban, suburban, or rural setting; the demographics of your community (race, age, national origin, etc.); the economy (manufacturing center, resort area, college town, etc.); and the character of your area; that is, are you in a friendly, open, dynamic environment, or a very traditional area with residents suspicious of anyone attempting to change things?

For a general idea of the poverty levels in your community, go to:

- Municipal planning offices (county, city, or borough, depending on your location)
- Chamber of commerce
- City hall or county commission
- Civic organizations such as Kiwanis and Exchange Club

- Social services (also known as family services, adult and child services, or department of human resources)
- Your Baptist association or state convention, which should have access to a wealth of demographic data about your area
- Baptist center

Be aware, however, that some organizations are not going to want to admit to the existence of poor in their area because it might reflect badly on the image of the town. A bad image would be bad for local business. And, the person might actually not know. So if on your first stop an official says, "Oh no, we don't have that problem here," do not take just that person's word. Continue with your assessment. By talking to a variety of sources, you can get a better picture of poverty in your community, and you can also get a better picture of how different groups view that poverty and its causes. This is especially important in maintaining sensitivity to people's culture and circumstances.

You will want to get a clear picture of poverty, but certain sources will just naturally be able to tell you about certain needs. If you are interested in the health needs of the poor, you would contact:

- Hospital administrator/social worker—especially emergency room social worker
- AIDS clinic
- Hospice
- Mental health center
- Fire department or ambulance service
- Doctors
- Pharmacists
- Public health nursing services/health department

Those with knowledge of literacy needs among the poor would be:

- Board of education
- Head Start program
- Adult education services
- School counselors/teachers
- Librarians
- Ethnic/language pastors
- Local businesses

To determine the ministry opportunities that address violence and the poor, visit with:
- Police or sheriff's department
- Fire department or ambulance service
- Victim advocacy group
- YMCA/YWCA
- Youth detention center
- Rape crisis/crisis counseling center
- Juvenile court
- Battered women's shelter

NOTE: Because of safety issues, a shelter for battered women and their children is usually in a secluded location to better protect the residents. If it is not possible for your group to meet at the shelter, ask a shelter staff member to meet you at another location for the survey.

Those with knowledge of the special needs of poor women and children include:
- School counselors/teachers
- Day-care centers
- Pediatricians/obstetricians
- Social services
- Homeless/battered women's shelters
- Rape crisis counselors
- Baptist centers
- Christian Women's Job Corps® sites
- YWCA

- Interdenominational community ministries
- Legal aid societies

There are a wealth of resources to turn to for information on hunger:
- Food banks
- Soup kitchens
- Food stamp and WIC program personnel
- Local restaurants
- Baptist center
- Local churches
- Community action agency

Two general resources that are often overlooked in surveys are the local newspaper reporters and the agricultural extension system staff. On a small newspaper you may be able to speak to the editor; on a larger newspaper you may wish to speak to a general news or city desk reporter. The extension system offers help to the public on everything from food safety to budgeting to raising gardens. Because they are community-oriented in their approach, extension staff also often serve on local boards and task forces to address area concerns.

After you have made a list of sites to visit, write down a list of questions. This will help you appear more serious about this endeavor, and save time for both your group and the people you are interviewing. Some people may wonder why you are talking to them. For example, a restaurant owner may think she knows nothing about local hunger. But you could ask, "Do people ever dig in your garbage for food? Do people ever come in asking what you do with unsold food at the end of the day? Do people come in looking underfed or saying they 'forgot' their wallet and can't pay for their meal?"

Sometimes the person you talk to may not know as much as some of the people who work the lower-level jobs in a place. For example, a restaurant owner may say to you, "No, I'm not aware of any hungry people." The waitress, if she overhears, may tell you of an elderly man who orders only coffee every morning, then asks other diners, "Could I have your leftovers for my dog?" She, however, has seen him then eat the leftovers ravenously as he stands in the parking lot. She is in a position to see the hunger around her. Likewise, a school bus driver sees poverty from a different vantage point than the superintendent of education of a huge school system.

AT THE INTERVIEW

When a group reaches a site where an interview has been planned (always on time), a designated person should take the lead in thanking the interviewee for her time, reminding those present what the objective of the interview is (finding out about the specific needs of the poor in the community) and then asking questions. Another person or persons may be designated to take notes. If you use a tape recorder, do so only with the permission of the interviewee. Either at the beginning or end of the interview, ask if you can pray for the person and his or her work. If the answer is no, do not make a big deal out of the refusal. (If the person gets to know you and your group better, he or she may end up calling you with prayer requests!)

The person you interview may be willing to give you only a few minutes as a formality. Others may be so excited that someone is actually interested that they want to take you out of the office on a tour! Do not vary from your schedule if you have other people waiting; but if you find a person keenly interested in working with you, by all means make another appointment to come back again.

As you interview, be aware that some secular agencies may fear that your interest in the poor is a pretext; that is, you are only pretending to want to minister in order to get close to people and then bully them into a religious conversion. Those who work with certain populations, such as criminal offenders or people with AIDS, may be especially wary. Others, including school officials, must worry about complaints concerning separation of church and state. Do not become discouraged if you meet such attitudes. Rather, be understanding and explain as many times as necessary that you wish to minister to the poor as a way of showing God's love, that you understand and respect the limitations the organizations work within, and that you do not wish to use your ministry to force or coerce anybody to do anything. With that laid to rest, you will find as you work patiently and compassionately, opportunities to share Christ will open up that you cannot imagine in the beginning of your ministry efforts.

WHAT DO WE DO AFTER THE TOUR?

When your tour of agencies and organizations is finished, your work has just begun. The group or groups of assessors should meet back together, possibly at the church, at an appointed time and share what they have learned. One person should be in charge of the debriefing, and another person should be the recorder. Everyone should have a chance to share what they learned.

The group then decides how to share that information with the church or association. You may wish to proceed by then having people in the church decide what ministries they wish to support or begin, or your group may have the responsibility of suggesting possible ministries. Either way is fine, as long as the newfound information doesn't end up buried in a file, never to be acted upon.

Write brief thank-you notes to persons interviewed and let them know any actions your church has decided to take. If no ministry activities are planned, but church members showed an interest in volunteering at the agency, share that also.

ASSESSMENT IN A NUTSHELL

1. Appoint a group or groups to do the assessment tour.
2. Make a list of agencies/individuals to interview.
3. Contact potential interviewees and ask for permission to visit with them. Explain what information you are hoping to gain and how much time you will take.
4. With your list of acceptances, make a schedule, including time for travel to and from each agency. Plan to spend a half hour at each site.
5. On the day of the tour, meet together and go over the schedule. Make sure the group has a leader and a note-taker. The note-taker should not be the same person as the leader. Remind group members not to make promises of assistance at this time.
6. Pray.
7. Conduct the assessment.
8. Meet back together at an appointed place and time to debrief. Have a leader and a recorder (again, not the same person).
9. Plan how to share the information with the church and begin the process of ministry.
10. Write thank-you notes to those interviewed.

AGENCY SURVEY FORM

Agency name: _____

Mailing address:_____

City, State, ZIP:_____

Telephone:_____ **Email:** _____

Web site:_____

Name of person interviewed: _____

Position: _____

What services do you offer?

What group or groups of people receive those services?

What have you identified to be the unmet needs of the people in the area you serve?

What plans do you have to begin services to meet those needs?

Are you facing any imminent changes in funding or personnel that would create a gap in your services?

What ways do you foresee that our church and your agency could work together?

Person conducting interview_____

Date of interview _____

Daytime telephone number of interviewer _____

Agency Survey Summary and Evaluation

How many agencies did we contact? _____

How many are good networking/referral sources? _____

How many geographic areas did our survey cover? _____

How many volunteers participated in the survey? _____

Do we need to schedule another survey for more information? ___

What needs did people mention most often?

1.

2.

3.

4.

5.

6.

7.

8.

Which of these needs can be met through our church's ministry to the poor?

1.

2.

3.

4.

5.

Follow-up Action Checklist

__√__ Follow-up Action (person responsible, completion date)

— _____

— _____

— _____

10

ADVOCACY

"Every person of faith has a special obligation to the poor and the powerless, and to seeking justice." Marian Wright Edelman, Children's Defense Fund

What is an advocate? According to Diana Garland, author of the book on child advocacy *Precious in His Sight,* "An advocate is one who stands up and speaks out for others. An advocate confronts injustice and supports just ways in which people can live together."[1] Let us revisit Bible passages quoted earlier that teach us what God wants of an advocate.

"Let justice roll on like a river, righteousness like a never-failing stream!" (Amos 5:24 NIV).

"To do righteousness and justice is more acceptable to the Lord than sacrifice" (Prov. 21:3 NKJV).

"It is a joy for the just to do justice, but destruction will come to the workers of iniquity" (Prov. 21:15 NKJV).

"Deliver those who are drawn toward death, and hold back those stumbling to the slaughter. If you say, 'Surely we did not know this,' does not He who weighs the hearts consider it? He who keeps your soul, does He not know it? And will He not render to each man according to his deeds?" (Prov. 24:11–12 NKJV).

"Happy is he who has the God of Jacob for his help, whose hope is in the Lord his God, who made heaven and earth, the sea and all that is in them; who keeps truth forever, who executes justice for the oppressed, who gives food to the hungry. The Lord gives freedom to the prisoners" (Psalm 146:5–7 NKJV).

"'Speak up and judge fairly; defend the rights of the poor and needy'" (Prov. 31:9 NIV).

As shown by the verses just cited, a concern for justice is not just pleasing to the Lord; it is one of God's requirements for the believer because it is a quality of God. In Psalm 146, God is shown to be the One Who gives justice to the oppressed, food to the hungry, and freedom to the prisoners. Securing justice in human relationships is therefore also the work of God. For God's followers to seek justice is even more pleasing to God than sacrifice. In these and other verses, the biblical witness makes a connection between suffering, oppression, and poverty. As shown in other chapters, many of the causes of poverty are rooted in a lack of justice. To be poor is almost always to be powerless, and the powerless are easily oppressed, for they have no voice. Those who have the ability must raise their voices in the cause of justice. Concern for justice must be actively shown by having the courage to speak out on behalf of the suffering.

Proverbs 31:9 exhorts us to defend the rights of the poor and the needy—again, the need to demand justice is linked to the poor and needy among us. The verse from Amos that likens justice to a powerful river or an ever-flowing stream must be understood from the context of the landscape where Amos and his listeners lived. Water is vital to life everywhere; but for an agricultural people in a land given to drought, an unfailing stream of water promises life and security. Is it any wonder that Amos would compare water to justice, which is also necessary for life and security?

The Bible also teaches us the outcomes of either seeking justice or not seeking it. Seeking justice brings joy to the righteous. The workers of iniquity—those who seek to pervert justice—can expect destruction, Proverbs says. And there is no use in trying to avoid our duty to be advocates by saying, "We didn't know." We might fool others; we might even fool ourselves. We will not fool the One Who weighs our hearts and keeps our souls. Ignorance was no excuse in the time the Scriptures were being written. How much less excuse do we have in the twenty-first century, when we have ample opportunities to learn how to help those in need?

THE POWER OF ADVOCACY GROUPS

North Americans have the blessing of being able to freely petition their governments and cultural entities, such as the media, with their concerns. Advocates can work in national or international groups, as do Amnesty International and Bread for the World, with a highly structured organization. Advocates can also work on the state or local level, in small groups, or individually. Even one voice can sometimes make a difference.

Since so many advocacy groups and efforts already exist, it is helpful for the advocate to first educate herself about what is currently being done. Others interested in advocacy in a certain area, such as homelessness, can form a network or give advice. The Internet is probably the quickest way to find people who share a concern. Merely looking at a Web site, however, may not give a person a true picture of a group's agenda. Viewing a Web site should be a starting point in researching advocacy issues. Contact the organization and ask if it has a mission statement, goals, or a vision statement that you can read. Find out how it is financed and what approaches it is willing to take to make its voice heard. Some groups are so certain of the justice of their views that they feel "the ends justify the means." Such an attitude can contribute to the problem rather than solve it.

If you find an advocacy group such as Bread for the World, find out if there are local chapters where you can go to find out the latest issues being addressed and meet your fellow advocates. If no chapter is in your area, perhaps you could start one. Even if that is not possible, an advocacy group can keep you connected with them through emails and phone calls. You will be told of upcoming legislation or media coverage affecting your issue and be given ways to impact the outcome.

The writer of Ecclesiastes said, "A threefold cord is not quickly broken" (Eccl. 4:12 NKJV). When you join your voice to those of others, and are educated about your issue, you can be a more effective advocate. And an advocacy group can help fight "negative information" which is a way of saying misinformation. For many years rumors have circulated via chain letters or word of mouth. Now the ability to receive email from people you have never met has multiplied the spread of these myths. Many Christians and other people of good intentions have been embarrassed when they have passed on something they thought was a fact, only to find out later it was an urban legend. Not only are they mortified, but their effectiveness as advocates is reduced because they have made themselves look foolish and gullible. Advocacy groups spend part of their time helping people distinguish between the truth and these modern myths. If you receive your information from a respected advocacy group rather than an anonymous mass email that's been passed around the Internet for months or years, you are less likely to be fooled.

As you join with others as advocates for the poor, do not overlook cooperating with the poor themselves. Those who have suffered in poverty have a unique perspective and a powerful motivation to help themselves and others. They can become their own best advocates.

A SINGLE VOICE

Sometimes no advocacy organization exists, or is not large enough to help you address an issue. Or perhaps you don't want to tackle a worldwide issue and win a Nobel Prize; you just want to help two homeless families you found living under a nearby bridge. You can be an advocate yourself. Consider that almost every great movement started with one person who enlisted a few other people of like mind. This small group grew into a movement that changed things. It did not always become a majority; but it became a force in the world.

Most likely when you start advocating for others, one of the first responses you will get is "Why don't you handle it yourself?" Take the example of the families living under a bridge. Especially if you have any financial means yourself, you will hear, "If you are so concerned, why don't you take care of them?" This is a legitimate question—to a point. Christ commanded us to sacrifice for the poor and needy. But this question is also a way for someone to pass the buck right back to you. When you have done all you can do, there will still be needs. Not only will there be needs for these two homeless families, but the causes of their homelessness—unemployment, drug abuse, domestic violence, illness, or whatever—will still exist. Other families will fall prey to those causes. Neither you, nor your church, can take care of everyone caught in the cycle of poverty. So there must be advocates to change the things that keep that cycle going.

In order to be a good advocate, you must have certain qualities, the first of which we have already touched on— knowledge. If you have actively ministered among the poor and oppressed, you have firsthand knowledge of the reality of their situation. While that is powerful, it is not enough. As stated in chapter 2, those who deal with making policies and laws need more than anecdotes of personal experience. They need facts and statistics to give them the Big Picture. You must be able to give that to them. It also helps to acquaint yourself with contradicting viewpoints so you will know how to answer objections and questions.

Another quality an advocate must have is the ability to communicate well. Thankfully, this is a skill that can be learned. You will get better with practice. If necessary, rehearse what you want to say with a friend who is a good communicator, or ask someone to read a letter you have written to make sure you have expressed yourself well. Part of being able to communicate is being able to respond with both firmness and gentleness. Some advocates seem to think that because they are on the side of the angels, they can act like devils. Yelling, calling people names, assuming that anyone who disagrees with them is either stupid or going straight to hell—such behavior damages not only the issue at hand, but the very name of Christianity. Jesus showed us it is possible to be both very firm and very loving. Modern advocates can also model a civilized approach that prevents discussion from being turned into heated argument. One young woman was discussing an issue with an elderly gentleman who seemed determined to put the worst interpretation on everything she said. After he made one rather silly accusation, she simply smiled and said, "Now you are being ridiculous." When he grew even angrier she murmured, "We shall just have to agree to disagree." It was difficult for him to continue arguing after that. The discussion did not bring the issue to a resolution, but the advocate's refusal to take offense or be rude kept the encounter at a civil level. Because of that, there was hope for future understanding.

Along with the qualities already mentioned, the advocate needs courage. Advocates are often unpopular. The Old Testament prophets were despised in great part because they dared tell Jewish society that it was disobedient to God's laws where the poor were concerned. Modern advocates often fare no better. Their treatment can run the gamut from being shunned at church to receiving death threats in the mail. Even advocates who have no reason to fear hostility may have to face that thing so many Americans fear—public speaking.

So why do it? Why even be an advocate if it's demanding and sometimes even frightening? I call your attention to the verses at the beginning of this chapter. It is what God commands. It is what God expects. And God will empower us to do what we are called to do.

"Fear thou not; for I am with thee: be not dismayed; for I am thy God: I will strengthen thee; yea, I will help thee; yea, I will uphold thee with the right hand of my righteousness" (Isa. 41:10 KJV).

"I can do everything through him who gives me strength" (Phil. 4:13 NIV).

CHILDREN AS ADVOCATES

Diana Garland wrote, "Children have a keen sense of fairness and justice. Children are aware of community and world issues and events. They worry about poverty, ecology and the fate of others. Children and youth can serve as powerful advocates for other children. The church can be a place to act on their concerns."[2]

We fall short of passing on Christian life and teachings to our children if we do not teach them about speaking up for justice for the poor and defenseless. Children and youth can be advocates in the following ways:

- Writing letters to the editor
- Doing projects and reports on a social issue
- Forming advocacy groups at school or church
- Speaking in church on a social issue
- Helping adults become aware of problems and needs of their peers
- Attending public meetings and speaking when appropriate
- Communicating their concerns with public officials

Some young people have become so devoted to advocacy for a certain cause, such as child slavery, that they have launched their own organizations or Web sites. They put their elders to shame with their knowledge, passion, and willingness to devote themselves to the suffering.

As we teach our children and teenagers to become advocates, we must, however, never lose sight of the fact that they are young and impressionable. Some adults must see and hear of horrors for themselves to believe they exist, or to be shaken from their complacency. Such knowledge could deeply upset a tenderhearted child. Children must be given knowledge at a rate appropriate for their development. They should be allowed to participate while still having their innocence protected.

In order to protect them, children should not be used as living props for a stunning visual effect. Some people on all sides of the political/moral spectrum feel justified in giving a child a sign almost as big as she is and having her march in a protest or stand in a picket line. They make sure the child is pushed in front of the TV camera so viewers can read the sometimes profane or spiteful messages and hear the child parrot whatever the adults have told her to say. A child should become an advocate for something she can understand in ways she can understand. She should be taught to be a Christlike advocate.

With that said, it should be noted that teaching children advocacy is a vital part of helping them learn compassion and courage through service to God. "Encouraging children to serve as advocates for others helps them develop spiritually."[3]

METHODS OF ADVOCACY

You can advocate for others in many ways, including:
- Writing letters to the media
- Writing editorials for newspapers, radio, or television
- Taking part in public forums such as city council, county commission, or school board meetings
- Contacting legislators
- Speaking on the issue in church or through social contacts
- Volunteering to serve on task forces or commissions to find solutions to the problem
- Starting a newsletter or Web site to inform people about the issue

You can email your legislators, but probably will not receive a personal reply unless you have included your name and physical address. To write a letter, use the following forms.

The Honorable _____
The United States House of Representatives
Washington, DC 20515

The Honorable _____
The United States Senate
Washington, DC 20510

Many people sign petitions, and these can be useful, as long as you know who is sponsoring the petition, how it is being used, and what is actually being said. Email petitions, while popular, are generally considered useless as a means of effecting change. So are form letters. Individual emails, however, can serve the same purpose as an individual letter. Letters should be legible and spelled correctly. Of course, you will always want to sign your name to a letter. Anonymous letters or those signed, "A concerned citizen" bear very little weight among either politicians or the media. If you care enough to write a letter, have enough courage to sign your name.

Whether you call, visit, or write a person, as an advocate you will always want to use good manners and a respectful tone. Writing a letter full of venom and then signing it "Your friend in Christ" does not impress the recipient (at least not in the way you want!). Keep visits brief and letters limited to one page. Focus and show that you are knowledgeable about the issue. While sometimes you may receive a polite brush-off, the time is likely to come when the person you have approached, whether a director of missions or a US senator, looks at you and says, "What exactly do you want me to do about this problem?" Be prepared with your answer. Say, "We want you to continue to fund this literacy program for another two years." Do not say, "We want you to fix things!" Believe it or not, most people in authority really would love to be able to just "fix things" if they could. They can't; that's why they need advocates to help them know what to do. They also need those advocates to say, "How can we pray for you?"

PRAYER STRATEGY

1. "Pray without ceasing" (1 Thess. 5:17 NKJV).
2. Pray about being an advocate.
3. Ask God to lead you to other advocates. Pray for wisdom and courage.
4. Pray for those who are dedicating their lives to being advocates for the poor.
5. Pray for the right words to say when you have an opportunity to speak up for others.
6. Pray that you will respond with love and patience when it would be easy to react with anger.
7. Pray for children to have opportunities to learn to be advocates.
8. Pray for those in offices of power that they will replace injustice with justice, complacency with action, selfishness with mercy.
9. Pray that through your advocacy, the poor will be helped, justice will be done, and God will be glorified.

[1]Diana Garland, *Precious in His Sight,* 2nd ed. (Birmingham, AL: New Hope Publishers, 1996), 22.
[2]Ibid., 35.
[3]Ibid.

11

MINISTRY IDEAS FOR CHILDREN AND YOUTH

"Even a child is known by his deeds, by whether what he does is pure and right" (Prov. 20:11 NKJV).

Teaching the young to serve the poor with compassion is as much a part of Christian nurture as teaching Bible stories and prayers. Here are some ideas that adults can use when leading the young in service to the poor.

IDEAS FOR YOUTH

1. Advocacy (see chap. 10 for a full discussion of advocacy).
2. Provide childcare at church so mothers can work, parents can look for jobs, etc.
3. Sack and deliver groceries at a food bank.
4. Operate a Web site that informs people about poverty issues and links people with resources.
5. Volunteer with an organization such as Habitat for Humanity.
6. Go on missions trips to poverty-stricken areas.
7. Create a multimedia presentation on some aspect of poverty for church or school.
8. Become a peer counselor or a tutor for younger children.

9. Assist in an English-as-a-second-language (ESL) ministry by creating visuals or helping students practice conversational English.

10. Lead recreation, crafts, or music at day camps and Bible schools for at-risk children.

11. Join environmental groups that focus on cleaning up trash and beautifying local areas.

12. Sort clothes and put together outfits at a clothing ministry.

13. Do yardwork for the sick, elderly, and disabled.

14. Produce a public service announcement for a ministry (food bank, tutoring program, etc.) and ask radio or TV stations to air it.

IDEAS FOR ADULTS AND CHILDREN

1. Collect things—food for a food drive, school supplies for an adopted school, toiletries for AIDS patients, etc.

2. Decorate grocery sacks for a food ministry.

3. Decorate paper bags for a sack lunch ministry, putting Bible verses and cheery pictures or stickers on them.

4. Make flash cards for a literacy ministry.

5. Draw posters for a churchwide emphasis on some ministry to the poor.

6. Make a bulletin board to promote the World Hunger Offering.

7. Make banks from milk cartons. Give the banks to church members to use in collecting change for a world hunger offering.

8. Help adults put up flyers and advertise ministries.

9. Memorize Bible verses, such as the ones quoted in this book, that teach about God's love for the poor.

10. Perform a puppet show, a skit, or a short drama about the church's responsibility to the poor.

11. Prayerwalk with adults around a school, community, Baptist center, or wherever the poor can be found.

TEACHING THE GOLDEN RULE

In teaching children and youth about ministry to the poor, there is a time for structured activity, such as working in the food bank, and there is a time for open-ended thought and reflection. Yes, it's good to take youth to clean up an elderly couple's overgrown yard. If those same youth, however, don't develop a deeper sense of compassion for the limitations of that couple, if they go away still lacking in genuine respect for them as fellow human beings loved by God, no real teaching has taken place. They will simply feel they have done a good deed that they can check off their list.

Likewise, the same children that on Sunday are diligently making flash cards for volunteers to use in an ESL ministry, on Monday may be mocking and ridiculing the immigrant children in their classrooms, and yet see no conflict in their behavior!

Practicing random acts of kindness is all to the good, but God's people should be practicing kindness with purposeful intent. They should understand on a spiritual, intellectual, and psychological level that the Christian has a calling to the poor because we are God's servants.

To truly raise up a generation of servants, the church must not only show children and youth all the different ways they can minister to people, but teach them why people are poor, how it affects a person to be poor, and how God wants them to treat the poor.

The basis for ministry to the poor is the Golden Rule: Do unto others as you would have them do unto you. This verse has been quoted so often and so tritely that it has become almost a mindless approach to ministry when actually, a great deal of consideration must be put into treating others as you would want to be treated.

For example, it seems obvious if a teenager is lacking in clothes, toiletries, and school supplies, he would want someone to provide these things. If the teenagers in your church were lacking the basics in life, they would want someone to help them. But, imagine the following scene. Some needy teenagers are called together for a party. The generous donors are at the party. The adults purchased gifts and the church youth group wrapped the presents and hand them out. The adults make a little speech about how they are called "unto the least of these." The teenagers open the gifts while the donors watch. They are urged to publicly show their appreciation for the gifts. They mumble their thanks and retreat hastily. The next day at school, the kids who received the gifts have to sit beside the same kids who brought the gifts. The humiliation is complete when one girl turns around in class and announces, "Hey, those clothes our church bought you guys look good!"

Now imagine those teenagers are put through this experience several times a year—when they begin school, at Christmas, Easter, etc. Some of them become so humiliated that they practically throw the gifts down and say, "Who needs your stupid stuff?" Others have adapted better, take the gifts casually, almost as something that was due to them.

This is not treating others as you would want to be treated; but every year, especially at Christmas, it seems well-meaning groups want their teenagers to learn how to minister by helping in situations where they come into contact with their lower-income peers or with lower-income adults. This is not appropriate; nor is it appropriate to have teenagers teaching adult reading and writing to people old enough to be their grandparents. When bringing children and youth into ministry situations, you must take into account what could be called the "embarrassment factor" of those being helped.

Everything you just read does not mean, however, that children and youth can't be involved in ministry. It does mean that ministry projects should go hand in hand with Bible study, Scripture memorization, and thoughtful discussion about poverty, justice, and the value of people in God's eyes. You can help young people develop a biblical sense of the worth of others. In doing so, they will develop a healthier sense of their own worth. If one day they face failure or rejection, as they will if they live long enough, they will remember those lessons taught about humanity being of more worth than "many sparrows."

EMBRACING YOUTHFUL ENTHUSIASM

While you work to be sensitive to the ways in which youth and children minister to the poor, also be aware that they may come up with some great ideas for ministry on their own. Don't automatically dismiss their ideas as too grandiose to work. God inspires young people, too. Their enthusiasm may lead them to new heights of serving God. For example, one high school group wanted to help with a local Christmas toy drive. They could have merely asked friends to bring toys to school and put them in a cardboard box. The group wanted to do more, however, and one of the teenagers secured a grant from a charitable foundation, a grant for several thousand dollars!

Young people can be self-centered and unaware, just as older people can. They can also be compassionate and brave, unselfish and creative, ready to give the best of themselves for something worthwhile. By including them in ministry, you have the opportunity to engage them in the most worthwhile endeavor of their lives—showing God's love to a world that is starving for that love to be shown in tangible ways.

RESOURCES

GENERAL RESOURCES

Books
What Every Church Member Should Know About Poverty by Bill Ehlig and Ruby K. Payne. Highlands, TX: aha! Process, Inc., 1999.
Framework for Understanding Poverty by Ruby K. Payne. Highlands, TX: aha! Process Inc., 2001.
Conspiracy of Kindness by Steve Sjogren. Ann Arbor: Servant Publications, 1993.

Organizations

American Bible Society
1865 Broadway
New York, NY 10023-7505
www.americanbible.org

Habitat for Humanity
121 Habitat Street
Americus, GA 31709-3498
www.habitat.org

International Mission Board
P. O. Box 6767
Richmond, VA 23230
www.imb.org

LifeWay Christian Resources
One LifeWay Plaza
Nashville, TN 37234
www.lifewaystores.com
www.lifeway.com

North American Mission Board
4200 North Point Parkway
Alpharetta, GA 30022-4176
www.namb.net

Volunteer Connection
P. O. Box 830010
Birmingham, AL 35283-0010
www.wmu.com/getinvolved/ministry/volunteer

Woman's Missionary Union
P. O. Box 830010
Birmingham, AL 35283-0010
www.wmu.com
www.wmustore.com

HUNGER RESOURCES

Organizations
Bread for the World
50 F Street NW
Washington, DC 20001
www.bread.org

HEALTH RESOURCES

Organizations
Baptist Nursing Fellowship
P. O. Box 830010
Birmingham, AL 35283-0010
www.wmu.com/getinvolved/ministry/bnf

International Parish Nurse Resource Center
205 Touhy, Suite 104
Park Ridge, IL 60068
1-800-556-5368
www.advocatehealth.com

CRIME AND VIOLENCE RESOURCES

Books
Leading Criminal Justice Ministry: Bringing Shalom, compiled by Betty Hassler. Nashville: LifeWay Press, 1998. Available through LifeWay Christian Resources or LifeWay Christian Stores.

Organizations
Prison Fellowship Ministries
1856 Old Reston Avenue
Reston, VA 20190
www.pfm.org

For training to minister to law enforcement/criminal justice professionals, contact:
Baptist General Convention of Texas
333 North Washington
Dallas, TX 75246-1798
www.bgct.org

For victim-related training and materials, contact:
Victory Network
526 Valley Road
Lowndesboro, AL 36752

WOMEN AND CHILDREN'S MINISTRY RESOURCES

Organizations
Christian Women's Job Corps
A Ministry of WMU
P. O. Box 830010
Birmingham, AL 35283-0010
www.wmu.com/getinvolved/ministry/cwjc

LITERACY RESOURCES

Books
Wonderful Words of Life by Cathy Butler. Birmingham, AL:
Woman's Missionary Union, 2000. Available from WMU,
SBC.

Organizations
ProLiteracy Worldwide (a merger of Literacy Volunteers of
America, Inc., and Laubach Literacy International)
1320 Jamesville Avenue
Syracuse, NY 13210
1-888-528-2224
www.proliteracy.org

National Institute for Literacy
1775 I Street NW, Suite 730
Washington, DC 20006-2401
Literacy hotline: 1-800-228-8813
www.nifl.gov

CULTURAL SENSITIVITY RESOURCES

Books

A Beginner's Guide to Crossing Cultures by Patty Lane. Ann Arbor: InterVarsity Press, 2002.

Thank you!

Your purchase of this book and other WMU products supports the mission and ministries of WMU. To find more great resources, visit our online store at www.wmustore.com or talk with one of our friendly customer service representatives at 1-800-968-7301.

WMU®
Discover the Joy of Missions℠
www.wmu.com